STRONG IN THE SPIRIT

BUILDING SPIRITUAL STRENGTH

MARK FOLEY

BALBOA.
PRESS

A DIVISION OF HAY HOUSE

Scripture taken from the New King James Version. Copyright © 1979, 1980, 1982 by Thomas Nelson, Inc. Used by permission. All rights reserved.

Balboa Press books may be ordered through booksellers or by contacting:

Balboa Press
A Division of Hay House
1663 Liberty Drive
Bloomington, IN 47403
www.balboapress.com
1 (877) 407-4847

Because of the dynamic nature of the Internet, any web addresses or links contained in this book may have changed since publication and may no longer be valid. The views expressed in this work are solely those of the author and do not necessarily reflect the views of the publisher, and the publisher hereby disclaims any responsibility for them.

The author of this book does not dispense medical advice or prescribe the use of any technique as a form of treatment for physical, emotional, or medical problems without the advice of a physician, either directly or indirectly. The intent of the author is only to offer information of a general nature to help you in your quest for emotional and spiritual well-being. In the event you use any of the information in this book for yourself, which is your constitutional right, the author and the publisher assume no responsibility for your actions.

Any people depicted in stock imagery provided by Thinkstock are models, and such images are being used for illustrative purposes only. Certain stock imagery © Thinkstock.

Print information available on the last page.

ISBN: 978-1-5043-3349-8 (sc)
ISBN: 978-1-5043-3350-4 (e)

Balboa Press rev. date: 06/18/2015

DEDICATION

This book is dedicated in loving memory to George and Mary Foley. Their love and support has been an anchor to me through the storms of life. They will continue to live forever in the hearts of their children and friends.

SPECIAL THANKS

- To everyone at Balboa Press that helped to make this book a reality.
- To Blake Atwood of EditFor.me (www.editfor.me.com), for his editing expertise.
- To my friends and loved ones for all of their encouragement and support.

CONTENTS

Introduction: Building Spiritual Muscles

What makes someone a strong Christian?

Do they never make mistakes?

Do they never give up?

Or have they learned much through life's experiences and now trust God in a greater way?

Story after story in the Bible gives us great insight into God's strategy to strengthen us. Consider these examples of those who were strong in the Spirit:

- Against all odds, Caleb says, "Let us go up at once, and possess it; for we are well able to take the land" (Num. 13:30).
- With fearless abandon, King David declares, "Who is this uncircumcised Philistine that he should defy the armies of the living God?" (1 Sam. 17:26).
- To his armor bearer, Jonathan commands, "Come let us go over to the garrison of these uncircumcised . . . for there is no restraint to the Lord to save by many or by few" (1 Sam. 14:6).

These men and countless others became strong in the Lord, but that's not how they began. They were just like you and me: men and women who believed in God.

By God's design, we all begin weak: "God has chosen the weak things of the world to confound the things that are mighty . . . that no flesh should glory in His presence" (1 Cor. 1:27–29). We are "the weak things," yet God desires to make the weak things strong. When the apostle Paul wrote, "Who through faith subdued Kingdoms . . . stopped the mouth of lions . . . out of weakness, were made strong" (Heb. 11:33–34), he was referring to the mighty men and women of God—further evidence that God chooses the weak then makes them strong. These powerful servants of God were not born that way, but they became that way. Along with trials and testing, their spiritual strength grew as a result of a deeper understanding of God.

The Close Connection Between Spiritual and Physical Strength

After years of pastoring and living for God and years of being a personal trainer, I've noticed a number of similarities between how God builds our spiritual strength and how the human body builds physical strength. Within the pages of this book, you will come to understand 10 life-changing correlations to bring clear perspective in living the Christian life. My hope is that you'll see your spiritual trials in a different light, and instead of viewing them as difficulties to endure; you'll see them as opportunities to increase your spiritual strength.

Our Heavenly Father is endeavoring to make us strong in the power of his Spirit, but just like weight training and working out, it's not always easy. Physical fitness is a process that takes a lot of hard work. We can't just join a gym, read a book, or visualize our new body with a positive attitude. If that's all that we do, our body will never change. It's only through the pain and difficulty of training that our bodies are actually strengthened.

Our spiritual lives are similar. We can't just join a church, read a new book, or visualize what we desire spiritually. It's a process, and one that we might not always understand. Without the right perspective and understanding of what to do, many of us settle for less than what God has for us. Some even give up the faith, believing that God isn't real or that he doesn't care, when in fact the opposite may be happening. God sees our weakness and leads us to strength. Challenging life moments are sometimes just God's way of strengthening us.

We need to understand God's ways. "They do always err in their heart, and they have not known My ways" (Heb. 3:10). When we don't understand God's ways, we usually presume the opposite. Instead of being encouraged to trust the Lord and allow his will to happen in our lives, we let in negative thoughts. We need to understand God's ways by gleaning insight and perspective from those that have gone before us in God's Word.

Your Spiritual Personal Trainer

For health, fitness, and strength conditioning, there's nothing like having a personal trainer. They provide experience and insight into muscle building, routines, and strategies. They instruct you on nutrition and cardiovascular health. Their desire is that your body reaches its full potential. So, consider this book your spiritual personal trainer, helping you to reach your full potential in the Spirit, and thus become the man or woman God intended you to be—one who lives from a place of strength, faith, and trust.

God provides us both the ability and the desire to accomplish his will. "It is God that works in you both to will and to do of His good pleasure" (Phil. 2:13). This is our workout. Through life's circumstances, we learn how to accomplish God's will for us, and we learn to desire His will. God desires to make us strong in the power of the Spirit, and he knows just how to make that happen. He's "building Spiritual strength" in us, to make us strong.

Many spiritual truths and insights come to us by digging through the Scriptures to understand how God truly sees things. The Lord calls this a royal and honorable task: "It's the glory of God to conceal a thing; but the honor of Kings to search a matter out" (Prov. 25:2). So let us seek to understand this process and allow God to make us "strong in the Spirit".

CHAPTER 1

THE NEED TO TRAIN:
ATTAINING OUR DESTINY

When you see someone weight lifting, what's your first impression?

Unless you're already familiar with the science behind lifting weights, you'd say what most people say: "He wants to build muscle."

You'd be half right though. Yes, we build muscles by placing more stress on them than they're used to handling, but when we lift weights, we're actually *breaking down* the muscle.

That's why it's painful. When we're lifting heavier weights than normal, our body yearns to stop, but if we push through the pain and refuse to quit, lifting that weight begins to get easier. If we continue to train, lifting the starting weight becomes effortless. We get stronger and our physical muscles grow. This added strength gives us the ability to do things we never thought possible (and this comes from a benchwarmer turned Captain of his high school football team). All athletes who want to excel know one thing for sure: if you want to get stronger, you must train.

The same is true of our life in the Spirit.

When we become believers, we start our spiritual training as the apostle Peter explains in 1 Peter 4:12. "Beloved, think it not strange concerning the fiery trial which is to try you, as though some strange thing is happening to you." Just as heavy weights build big muscles, trials build big spiritual muscles. That's just the way it is.

I'd like to say that there's an easier way, but there's not. Trials burden us, they make life difficult for us emotionally, physically, and spiritually, and though the goal is to strengthen us, our trials usually feel like they're actually breaking us down.

Enduring trials often does weaken us. If we're honest with ourselves, we'll admit to giving up, or at least wanting to give up many times. Going through difficulties is never easy, but sometimes this is the way God works in our lives.

The truth is though, God has been working in our lives from conception: "And now, says the Lord that formed me from the womb to be His servant" (Isa. 49:5). God had a plan for us in mind when he made us, and everything we've experienced in our lives is designed to shape us into the person God has destined us to be.

Training with Bears and Lions

King David was destined to slay a giant, so as a young boy God sent him into training. When the sheep he tended came under attack by a bear and a lion, David had to decide whether to run away or stand and fight. Defending the sheep should have cost him his life, but something miraculous happened. As this young man stood in faith, believing that was what God wanted him to do, *God showed up.* The Holy Spirit came upon David, and he killed both the bear and the lion. The Spirit gave David abilities beyond his own human strength.

David's spiritual strength and trust in God were growing. God was strengthening David through trials. Then, when David reached his life's defining moment and heard Goliath's taunts, David wanted to fight. Why? Because he knew God would show up if he did.

When David was brought before King Saul, the king basically said, "You can't do it. He'll kill you." David's response was simply an explanation of the training God had already brought him through. "And David said unto Saul . . . 'There came a lion and bear, and took a lamb out of the flock . . . I caught him . . . and slew him. Thy servant slew both the lion and the bear: *and this uncircumcised Philistine shall be as one of them.* The Lord delivered me out of the paw of the lion and bear, and he will deliver me out of the hand of this Philistine'" (1 Sam. 17:34–37, emphasis added).

David didn't see Goliath. Instead, he saw what God had previously taught him. David had been training for that moment without even realizing it. This young boy accomplished something epic that no one else dared to do simply because he had allowed God to train him.

We need to allow God to train us today and to give us victory over present battles so that we will be better prepared for what life may throw at us in the future. This account of King David's life is a victorious example of God's desire to bring us through present battles while preparing us for greater ones to come.

I can imagine David returning from the slaughter of the Philistines that day, with Goliath's sword in one hand and his severed head still dripping blood in the other, standing before King Saul. This is the picture that the Enemy of our souls is scared to death of: God's people being trained for their destinies, then fulfilling them.

What If David Had Stopped Training?

Imagine that David had refused to stop the lion and the bear from attacking his sheep. There's a good chance that every one of his brothers had taken a turn watching that same group of sheep, and it's possible that the same bear and lion had come by for a nice snack as every one of his brothers had run away in fear. David could have even heard of these infamous animals his entire life. It would have been easy for him to think, "Why should I risk my own life for a few sheep?"

Though David's killing of Goliath is what history reveres him for, I believe this earlier story about David protecting the sheep is much more important. Had he run away from this earlier fight, he would not have been prepared to fight Goliath and win. Had he run away from that bear and that lion, I also don't believe God would have chosen him to be king.

God chose David to be King because of his heart. When Jesus told the parable of the Good Shepherd, he talked of the hireling who ran away when the sheep were threatened. The Good Shepherd, by contrast, defended the sheep at the risk of his own life. Then Jesus declared, "I am the Good Shepherd." This is the heart of God, and this is what Jesus and David had in common. David was literally the good shepherd. That's the reason David was a man after God's own heart; and that's why he was chosen. David was chosen out of obscurity because of his actions. "I have chosen thee in the furnace of affliction" (Isa. 48: 10).

Fiery trials give us great opportunities to grow in faith and find favor with God. The story of Joseph is a good example. Joseph refused Potiphar's wife's advances and was sent to jail. While in jail, he interpreted dreams that eventually brought him before Pharaoh. Imagine if Joseph had given in to

Potiphar's wife's advances. He probably would have never gone to prison. Imagine if he had been mad at God in prison and had refused to interpret his cellmate's dreams. Joseph never would have been brought before Pharaoh, so Egypt and his family would have died of starvation. The godly choices we make during the trials of life increase our spiritual strength and lead us to the victorious destiny the Lord has planned for us.

What are we missing out on by refusing to stand in faith where we are right now? What battles are we running away from? What training are we refusing to endure? What Goliath will we never defeat? What kingdom that we may be destined to rule will never even materialize?

If you feel like you're being stressed beyond your ability, it could be that God wants to strengthen you and give you his ability. If life feels painful to the point that you want to give up, it's because life *is* just plain hard and sometimes beyond our ability to endure. We need the miracle of God's ability.

The Christian life can be very difficult at times because the society we live in is often opposed to it. "The kingdom of God suffers violence and the violent take it by force" (Matt. 11:12). Society at large mocks us for investing in the Kingdom of God with our money, talent, passion, and zeal. At times, even our own logic says, "This doesn't make any sense. What am I doing?" We step out in faith and fall flat on our faces, and we think,

"Is this even real?" All the while God is calling to us: "Come on! Keep going! You can do it!" Jesus stands at the finish line saying, "Look at me. You've got this. You can do this!"

In 1 Peter 4:12, the apostle Peter (who endured a number of trials himself), says, "Think it not strange concerning the fiery trial, which is to try you as though some strange thing is happening to you." Through Peter, the Lord tells us *not* to be surprised when these trials come. He says that they will come and that they are designed to test us.

In the midst of trials, it's very easy to get overwhelmed and allow ourselves to get mad at God and others because life doesn't seem fair—but that's just the way life is sometimes. It wasn't fair that Jesus had to go to the cross, and sometimes it's not fair for us. It's like a personal trainer who pushes his client way beyond his ability and seems like a heartless slave driver, then months later the trainee pushes back tears while praising the trainer for helping him become more than he ever could have been on his own.

God works to make us great so we can fulfill our destiny. We are all destined for greatness, but we are not all chosen. "For many be called, but few chosen" (Matt. 20:16). We are being called to greatness as sons and daughters of God, and we are kings and priests of this heavenly calling. Will we trust the Lord through the fiery trials and allow him to mold us into great men and women of God? We are in training to become all that God desires us to be. We can either accept that fact and wholeheartedly enter into the training, or we can attempt to reason away why things are the way they are. That choice is up to each of us.

Choose greatness! Choose God!

Our physical bodies need fitness training to stay healthy, become stronger, and live longer. Obesity, diabetes, and other ailments reveal the dangers of not training. Our Spirit also needs training to become stronger so that we can attain our destinies. Giving in to every temptation, allowing hurts to embitter us, and giving up on God altogether reveal the dangers of not allowing our spirits to be strengthened. God has a destiny for us, and it is more beautiful than we could ever imagine. God is bringing us to that place, and on the way he is preparing us. God had a destiny for the children of Israel when they left Egypt, and it was called "a land flowing with milk and honey," a virtual oasis and paradise in the middle of the desert. That's what our Father in heaven is doing for us. He loves us and wants to strengthen us so that we might possess our "Promised Lands."

CHAPTER 2

MUSCULAR DEVELOPMENT: FAILURE IS NECESSARY

Weightlifters need a spotter from time to time. This person ensures the safety of the weightlifter, especially on exercise equipment like the bench press. After training for a while, a lifter on the bench press may not be sure if he has enough strength for one more repetition, but brings the weighted bar down to his chest anyway. Then with whatever strength remains, he pushes. He gets to the halfway point, and then barely to the three-quarter point, but his arms begin to shake. The bar stops in mid-air. His last lift is about to fail, and the heavy bar may come crashing down upon him—were it not for his spotter, who assists the lifter to finish his last lift.

That's called "going to failure," and it's the most effective way to build muscle because it shocks every muscle fiber engaged in the exercise. Simply put, the muscle *must* give everything it has, but it's still not enough, so the lifter fails to accomplish his last repetition. The lifter has purposefully pushed the muscle beyond its ability.

The muscle actually grows during recovery, the time that passes between workouts. The muscle is forced to create new fibers to keep up with the new demand put on it. While your muscle rests, imagine that it's having a conversation with itself: "This guy is crazy. We gave everything we had. It's still not nearly enough, and he just keeps doing it. We need some help!" This is when the miraculous creation of new muscle fibers occurs.

We need to create spiritual muscles if we are going to get spiritually stronger. To do that, failure and the fear of failure cannot be allowed to be a deterrent. Failure has caused many to leave the faith, and it has caused countless others to lose their passion and trust in God. At times we're hurt because we expected God to come through for us. At other times we're angry with others who seemed to have gotten away with what they did to us. Then there are those times when we do things we regret, like committing sinful actions or living a life of lukewarm commitment, where we're excited about the Lord in church, but not much different from the unsaved community when we leave. Failures in our Christian walk show up in many different ways, but that doesn't mean that we are a failure; it only means that we have failed at some very difficult task. Living the Christian life is the most difficult endeavor known to mankind, and having an understanding of God's grace and our Heavenly

Father's great love for us is the only thing that gives us a fighting chance.

Yes, we fail, but we are far from failures.

There are many misconceptions concerning failure's place in our spiritual lives. Let's take a look at one of the Bible's colossal failures, whom God also later entrusted to start his church, the apostle Peter. Remember when Peter told Jesus he would lay down his life for him? Jesus then replies, "I tell you, Peter, the cock shall not crow this day before you shall three times deny that you know me" (Luke 22:34). That's exactly what happened.

After the death of our Lord, Peter goes back to fishing. In other words, Peter fails God, then goes back to doing what he did before meeting the Lord. He must have thought to himself, "I am such a pathetic failure. I give up." After all, that's exactly what he did. Peter followed Jesus passionately and when his expectations didn't materialize, he quit. If we are honest with ourselves, we can admit to sometimes feeling the same way: confused that after passionately following the Lord, bad things still happened.

Can we even begin to imagine what Peter must have gone through? He loved Jesus and had spent three years giving his all. With the encouragement of the Lord, Peter had walked on water—what great faith! When the Lord asked the disciples who they thought he was, Peter said, "You are the Son of God." Jesus told Peter that

11

his Father in heaven revealed that to him—what great revelation! Then, when Peter told Jesus he would lay down his life for him, the Lord says, "This very night you will deny even knowing me." Then comes that moment in time when the rooster crowed and Peter's eyes met with Jesus, and instantly Peter remembered what the Lord had said. "And Peter said: 'Man, I know not what you say.' And immediately the cock crowed. And the Lord turned, and looked upon Peter . . . and Peter went out and wept bitterly" (Luke 22:60–62).

Peter was brought to a place of failure, and if that wasn't enough it gets worse. They crucified Jesus and Peter goes back to fishing. Now it's definitely over, and if the story ends there Simon Peter remains true to his name: "a reed shaken in the wind." He would have forever been known as the one who stood beside Jesus when things were good, but ran away when things got bad.

But that's not where the story ends. Jesus is only in the *middle* of forming Peter into a "rock." Peter is being changed from weakness to strength. Just like when the muscle is resting and saying, "We need help," Peter—maybe for the first time— is beginning to understand his own need for help.

Failure is designed to show us our need of God's help. We can't do it on our own, and that's the whole reason God chooses the weak, so that no flesh can glory in his presence. When we fail, we understand what we are able to accomplish in our own strength. Then when God restores us and uses us, we understand that it's the Lord who does great things through us.

Nothing breaks our self-sufficiency, pride, and ego like failure. We are so bent on our ability to accomplish things, even good things, that we can be crushed when they fail. We see it as a reflection upon us. We don't like to lose at any endeavor, and failure is like losing. We don't like feeling as though we're not good enough or don't have what it takes, but when it comes to the spiritual life, *we don't have what it takes.*

It's like salvation. We don't have what it takes to be forgiven of sins and assume a right standing with God. "For what the law could not do in that it was weak through the flesh, God sending his own son . . . condemned sin in the flesh" (Romans 8:3). What we could not do, Jesus did for us. When it comes to the spiritual world, it's like walking on water: we step out in faith and believe. We have no guarantees that it's true, yet we believe.

So it is with becoming strong in the Spirit, because it's the power of God doing something we cannot. This is why the apostle Paul says, "For when I am weak, then am I strong" (2 Cor. 12:10). What he's saying is that when I realize that I don't have what it takes, then I can do all things through Christ who strengthens me. God parted the Red Sea, held back the Jordan River, slew Goliath, and raised Jesus from the dead. And it was God who performed all of the miracles through the disciples in the book of Acts.

If we can learn to trust God *even in failure*, we begin to transcend the physical world and enter the spiritual. We stop thinking we can do it and start believing God can do it. Instead of knowing truths in our minds that we have read and believed to some extent, we experience these truths and know them to be true deep in our hearts. Our trust in God becomes immovable because Jesus comes to us in failures and lifts us back up. We become more certain of his reality. God's desire is not that we do everything perfect and earn some standing before him like we deserve it. He wants us to trust him, even if he gives us more than we can possibly handle.

If we endure and don't totally give up, what we first notice through failure is God's beautiful, amazing, compassionate love for us. When the women arrived at Jesus's tomb, the angel said to them, "Jesus is risen . . . go tell the disciples and Peter" (Mark 16:6–7). Can we even begin to imagine how Peter must have felt when he heard that? His heart must have leapt for joy. Jesus wanted Peter to know how much he still loved him. It didn't matter one bit that Peter had failed the Lord and had given up because Jesus loved him unconditionally, just like he loves us. Peter's story was far from over—as is ours.

So after the Lord is resurrected, he looks for Peter, and the Lord knows right where to find him: in his place of failure, back at fishing. Jesus calls to him in love like he did the first time, "Did you catch any fish?" Peter replies with a simple no. "Cast your net on the right side and ye shall find." And again, just like the first time, the net is so full of fish it nearly breaks. Peter realizes it is the Lord and jumps into the sea to go see him. They have a wonderful reunion, and the Lord again says to him, "Follow me." Peter picks up right where he left off with the same God and the same calling, but this time with a renewed and stronger faith.

So it is in our failure that the Lord calls to us again. Failure can seem like death because it's a spiritual death. Our faith is crushed and we're not sure how to feel. Ashamed of ourselves, mad at God, furious with others—there are a million ways to fail and spiritually die, but it is designed to change us. "Except a corn of wheat fall into the ground and die, it abides alone; but if it dies it brings forth much fruit" (John 12:24). The Lord is saying that if a seed never dies, it will never grow into what it was destined to be.

Though growth is always a painful process that we fail at more times than not, growth through failure always produces something beautiful. Everything God wants us to become is directly linked to us dying to certain things in our lives, and failure is the path to getting there.

Take pride for instance. God is trying to produce humility in our lives so our pride has to die, and it's never a pretty sight. People will take credit for the things we do, or they'll lie about us, or we might even become financially stressed or shunned by our friends and loved ones. We can lash out, or we can swallow our pride and understand that God sees everything. Pride dies within us, and love, humility, and grace begin to grow in its place—the fruits of the Spirit. This is what the Lord is referring to in the Scripture when he says, "That it brings forth much fruit." Many times in this process we fail, but the Lord always comes to us and picks us back up.

When we first became believers, Jesus came to us as a risen savior, and we experienced all of our sins being forgiven. What a miracle that was! We can recall feeling immensely loved. But when the Lord comes to us in failure, it's more like when he stood at the tomb of Lazarus and said, "I am the resurrection, and the life; he that believes in me, though he were dead, yet shall he live" (John 11:25). By experiencing God's power and understanding his commitment to us, we are strengthened. We see God's love for us like the prodigal father running to embrace his wayward son. We grow in maturity and understand like Joseph did that the Enemy meant this for evil, but God meant it for good. We understand our own limitations and need for God. Our spiritual muscles begin to find the help they need and we become spiritually stronger. Now when the Enemy tries to intimidate us like Goliath, we say bring it on! We go on the offensive. Whether it's what the Enemy tries to keep us from doing or what we're doing that we shouldn't (or any number of other things), we start believing beyond what we see and consequently become stronger in the Spirit. We trust that God loves us and knows what he is doing, even (and especially) if we don't.

Just look at Peter. The Lord comes to him in his failure and Peter is restored and stronger than ever. After the Lord showed himself for forty days and is taken up in their presence, Peter—the one who had verbally denied Christ, repeatedly—*takes over.* He called for a vote to replace Judas and they did. After Pentecost, Peter declared Jesus to a great crowd and three thousand were converted on the spot. Then he prayed for a lame man right in front of the temple, after which the lame man leapt to his feet and walks into the temple with them. As soon as everyone saw the lame man walking, they came running, and Peter preached his second sermon. He was then arrested by the temple guards, but not before five thousand more believed. The very next morning, Peter's brought before Annas the high priest and all of the other Jewish elders, rulers, and scribes. This is the same group Jesus stood before who ultimately sentenced him to death. Peter then preached his third sermon, and it was a scorching finger-pointer. "Be it known unto you all, and all the people of Israel, that by the name of Jesus Christ of Nazareth, whom you crucified, whom

God raised from the dead, even by him does this man stand here before you whole" (Acts 4:10).

What happened to Peter? Before, he was afraid of a couple of people out in public, but now he stands before the ones who crucified the Lord and roars boldness like a lion. He's grown spiritually stronger, and it has everything to do with experiencing failure in a major trial and allowing the Lord to change him. On the very night he denied the Lord, Peter promised, "I would never leave you. I will die for you." But in his own strength he failed. Yet when God restores him and uses him powerfully, Peter essentially says, "Don't look at me! I didn't heal him! It was Jesus!" His source of strength had changed, and only failure can accomplish that. That's what it's designed to do. Failure does not exist to derail us or make us give up, but to increase our faith so we can become spiritually stronger. Though it feels like failure may break us, it actually makes us, as we learn from it and draw closer to God.

We need a new perspective when it comes to failure. When Thomas Edison was asked about his thousands of failures while creating the incandescent light bulb, his response was unexpected. He effectively said, "I didn't fail. I discovered many ways that it wouldn't work, but I only needed to find one way that it would." He learned something from every failure, and that eventually led him right to his discovery.

Learning from our failures today leads us to a deeper discovery and understanding of God.

As we live for God and experience failure, it would serve us well to have the mindset of a major league batter. They can fail to get on base seven out of ten times, but instead of feeling like a failure, they're considered pretty good with a .300 batting average. It's all about perspective. What is God trying to show us through these failures? What is he teaching us about himself as he helps us through them? These are the questions we should be asking, not, "How could you let this happen to me God?"

We have to learn to trust God. These are just God's ways of teaching us. We're not failing—we're just discovering ways *not* to do things. In the process, we discover how true God's Word is and how beautiful God's grace is. The apostle Paul was familiar with failure when he wrote, "For I know that in my flesh dwells no good thing: for the will is present with me, but how to perform that which is good I find not. For the good that I would, I do not: but the evil that I would not, this I do" (Romans 7:18–19). Paul is saying that he doesn't do what he should and at the same time he does what he shouldn't. It sounds like he failed just as much as we do, and yet he is one of the greatest of Christian theologians. We all fail, and the Bible is full of examples of great men and women who have done the same.

God encourages us to get back into that good fight of faith. Just look at the story of David running away from King Saul. On two occasions

Saul was delivered into David's hands to show David that God was in control. Unfortunately, David tired of hiding and went to live with the enemies of God. David was so confused that he complained and threw a tantrum when he wasn't allowed to go kill the people of Israel in the battle that actually took both Jonathan and King Saul's lives. Then, when David and his men returned home, everything was gone, including their families. That was the last straw, and David's men were about to kill him. At this point, David came to his senses and prayed to God. He could have laid there in self-pity and have been stoned to death by his own men, but he chose to turn to God. David remembered that God was good, and that God had a plan for his life, and he encouraged himself in that. God told David to go get them and recover all, and that's exactly what happened. It was just a short time after this that King Saul's crown was placed on David's head as King of Judah, and eventually all of Israel.

King David learned how *not* to do things through experiencing grave personal failure while living with the enemies of God. We fail, but we're not failures. We're fighting the good fight of faith, and God is proud of us! God is saying the same thing to us that he said to David. Don't give up, but instead get up, pursue, and recover all! The fulfillment of our destiny is right around the corner.

CHAPTER 3

THE TRANSFORMATION: TRUSTING GOD

Transformation begins with the training routine. This day-after-day commitment to working hard—without seeing immediate results—starts with an assessment. The trainer takes you through a battery of conditioning exercises and evaluates your performance to discover your strengths and weaknesses. A training regimen is then developed and implemented to enhance all of your major muscle groups. Regardless of how effective the routine is or how motivational the trainer might be, the client only gets out of it what they put into it. Faithful dedication and passionate effort will result in a great transformation, but a half-hearted approach won't see much change at all. "No pain, no gain" is not a cliché in this arena—it's a way of life.

God desires us to become likewise spiritually transformed. He wants us to assess our current spiritual condition, trust him as our trainer, and endure the training he has developed and implemented for us. One of our problems is that we often have a wrong assessment of ourselves. Sometimes we assume that because we are good at praying for people, leading Bible studies, have great insight into the Word of God, or are gifted at winning souls to the kingdom, that we are strong believers. But at the same time we are easily beset by habitual sin, angry with God, or offended by others. We don't see our weakness because we think we are strong.

It's not what we do outwardly that makes us spiritually strong; it's who we are inwardly. We are as strong as we are like Jesus. Christ forming in us is what God's training was designed to accomplish. Spiritual strength can be summed up in one word: Jesus! He is the firstfruits, the first of many sons to come in the same image.

"To them that love God, to them that are called according to his purpose . . . to become conformed to the image of his son, that they may be the firstborn among many brethren" (Rom. 8:28–29). Jesus walked in the flesh as a man and showed us how to live the Christian life. He walked in love and mercy and showed strength and character. He acted in faith before God in every situation that came his way. Our main pursuit in life should be to act godly in whatever situation or trial we find ourselves in. Our failure to do so should be a sign to us of our weakness and our need for God to strengthen us.

Jesus is not dead, but he is alive in the form of the Holy Spirit living inside us. The Bible speaks of the Trinity as three-in-one, which means that God became man and dwelt among us. Jesus is God incarnate. The Holy Spirit is the creative power of God living inside each of us who profess Christ as Lord. The indwelling Spirit of God wants expression in our lives, and the godlier we act in life's situations; the more Jesus lives through us. The apostles were fortunate enough to have seen Jesus in person, but unfortunately we must live by faith, believing that Jesus is the Son of God. To the extent that we believe and give our lives to living by his teachings is really the amount of faith we have. So the weight we give to doing godly things in our lives is the amount of faith we have in God. If we want more faith, we just have to believe more and act upon what the Lord teaches. Of course, the only way to believe more is to trust that God's word is true. Trusting God through the training he has developed for us is the key. Think of it like a test we have to pass to get to our destiny, and if we fail we have to keep taking it until we pass. Look at Joseph's life.

Nothing in the Scriptures should lead anyone to believe that Joseph did anything wrong. He had an amazing prophetic dream from God himself that absolutely came true, and all Joseph did was tell his closest loved ones about the dream. His siblings and father were the ones with the problems. Joseph loved his family, and when the dream came true and Joseph revealed himself to his brothers, he embraced them and wept. When they threw him in the pit and pulled him out only to sell him to a caravan, the thought of his brothers doing that to him must have broken his heart.

Can we even begin to imagine how Joseph must have felt as he watched his brothers growing smaller and smaller in the distance until they were out of sight, fully realizing he'd been sold as a slave by his own brothers? How devastating that must have been. Joseph's life and dreams had been shattered, but unlike most, he continued to trust God. He acted godly in whatever situation God put him in. He became a blessing to Potiphar, and after being falsely accused, he became a blessing in jail. He then became a blessing to Pharaoh and all of Egypt.

Joseph endured heart-wrenching situations, but something was going on behind the scenes in the Spirit. God had taken an obscure little man from an obscure little family and had made him second to Pharaoh. God's route was the only path to getting there. Joseph even verbalized this when he said to his brothers, "What you meant for evil, God meant for good." Joseph kept passing the tests of trusting God, and his constant faith brought him right to his destiny. Likewise, trusting God where we are right now will lead us to our destiny.

It wasn't until Joseph saw his brothers bow down before him that he remembered the dream. Obviously, this was not Joseph's plan for making his dream come true, but it was God's. Many of us have dreams of what we feel God has put upon our hearts, and we get there by acting godly whenever we get the chance and trusting God no matter what happens. Of course, it's not easy. Just look at all of the hardship Joseph endured, but in the end it was all worth it. Imagine what the seven years of famine must have been like for Joseph, as everyone who wanted food had to bow down to him. Every time his brothers come for grain, I can hear Joseph laughing while saying, "Hey boys, remember that dream?" as they wipe dust off of their knees. Every time Potiphar visits and spends the entire time apologizing for the horrible injustice he did to Joseph, I can hear Joseph saying, "I guess you can't always believe everything your wife says." My favorite would be whenever Potiphar's wife comes by and exclaims, "I knew you were the real deal because only a man of God could resist me." Joseph was glad that he didn't give up on God, and we will be too.

Just like a physical training routine encompasses all of the major muscle groups, God's training also encompasses the major areas of our lives. Trust, humility, love, and hope are just a few examples of what God wants to strengthen in us. We go through trials or blessings that make us feel the opposite of these, and the goal is to rise above the situation and act godly. It's not just about passing the test and acting like Jesus would, but it's what you learn about yourself and about God while going through the trial that actually transforms you.

The easiest way to explain this is to give an example. Just look at Jacob, the deceiver. He deceived his father out of the blessing due the first-born son and runs away, but he gets a taste of his own medicine from his Uncle Laban. After working for seven years so he can marry Laban's daughter Rachel, Laban essentially tells Joseph, "I forgot to tell you that Leah gets married first. Sorry." Some of what we endure is so that we can experience what others have experienced because of our actions. Jacob felt cheated and lied to by Laban, and that is exactly how he had previously made his father and brother feel. Often we don't stop to consider what our actions do to others, and yet the Lord says, "When you do something unto the least of these, you do it to me." So, we should stop to consider.

Jacob then began realizing he was a deceiver and that his actions hurt others. He was receiving a revelation—of himself. He was also getting a revelation of God. God met with him and changed his name to Israel, "prince of God." Jacob was receiving a revelation of God's grace and how much God truly loved him. What he learned by going through God's training changed him from the inside out.

Understanding and trusting in God's love for us should be our paramount goal. Jesus was with the Father and knew that love, and it enabled him to trust God in spite of whatever he had to endure, including the cross. God wants to bring us to the point that we see him looking at us with so much love that he can't take his eyes off of us and for us to be looking at him with so much love that we can't take our eyes off of him, so that everything around us fades and only our trust and love in God remains.

This is how it must have been for Enoch. "And Enoch walked with God: and he was not, for God took him" (Genesis 5:24). They must have been so in love that God couldn't take it anymore, so he grabbed Enoch from off the face of the earth.

I love that. God must be very passionate for us. That's the God I serve. God knows that the closer we are to him, the stronger we will be spiritually and the more we will come to know him and fall deeper in love with him. Trusting God while enduring the trials of life and knowing that he has a plan for us draws us closer to him.

Of course, trusting God through difficult trials is much easier said than done, because trials usually involve pain, surrender, and dying to self. Trials provide us a place to become more like Jesus while at the same time entering into his sufferings. This is the place where a compassionate heart is created. When we tell someone that we understand what he or she is going through even though we've never experienced anything similar, our understanding is superficial. In all honesty, we really don't understand. We can throw some helpful Scriptures their way and try to console them, but that's about it.

Only when we've gone through similar difficulties can we look them in the eyes and say, "I know exactly how you feel," and share with them how God has helped us. Why do you think Christians who have been in jail are so powerful in prison ministries? Because they have been there and truly know what it's like. This is one of the reasons that God had to become a man: he had to know what being human was like so he could genuinely tell us, "I know exactly how you feel." Jesus was in all ways tempted like us, but didn't sin. He suffered trials and pain and suffering. Not only that, but he showed us how to endure such hardships. He's our example. The greatest blessing is that he prays and intercedes for us, and he knows exactly how we feel when we come to him in prayer. What a great comfort that is.

The prophet Ezekiel knew about the captives in the following verse, but it wasn't until he sat where they sat that he truly understood what they were going through. "Then I came to them of the captivity at Telabib, that dwelt by the river Chebar, and I sat where they sat, and remained there astonished among them seven days" (Ezekiel 3:15). We would likewise be astonished at what so many people around us are enduring if we just took the time to see through their eyes.

Nehemiah is the perfect example. When he came to Jerusalem and saw how bad things were, he essentially said, "Look at the distress *we are* in." Nehemiah himself wasn't in distress. He was living large in a palace with the King, but he put aside his convenience and entered into his people's suffering. That is a perfect example of Jesus, and a perfect example of what God is trying to do in our hearts: strengthening us to have more compassion for the lost, the less fortunate, and the brokenhearted. That's becoming like Jesus.

Remember the Scripture the Lord read when he began his public ministry? "The Spirit of the Lord God is upon me; because the Lord has anointed me to preach good tidings to the meek, He has sent me to bind up the brokenhearted, to proclaim liberty to the captives, and the opening of the prisons to them that are bound . . . to give to them beauty for ashes, the oil of joy for mourning, the garment of praise for the Spirit of heaviness" (Isaiah 61:1–3). That's who Jesus is, and that's what he wants us to become. All of this training in life is to accomplish that. Jesus wants to live through us and change the world. He can do it if we'll just trust him and believe. When we truly trust God, we are truly transformed.

CHAPTER 4

HEART TRAINING: FINDING GOD

The human heart is the most important muscle in the body. With every beat, the heart pumps freshly oxygenated blood through the arteries, bringing life to the entire body. The heart needs to endure cardiovascular training, which works to increase the heart's strength by increasing the heart rate.

The goal in any cardio training is to raise the heart rate and keep it there for at least thirty minutes. Brisk walking and running will accomplish that, as well as all of the machines in the cardio room at the gym. In the early 80s, aerobics was the cardio craze. Today, it's Zumba. By forcing the heart to beat faster, we increase its need for oxygen. We begin to breathe faster and more deeply, which exercises our lungs. We also perspire, which releases harmful toxins.

The benefits of heart training are endless. It burns calories, so many do it for weight loss. Athletes do it for endurance training so they can remain strong while others around them tire. Others find a sense of relief from the stress of life and enjoy when their endorphins kick in, commonly referred to as a "runners high."

But the most important thing happening is that the heart is being trained to function better and last longer. All other training seeks after physical fitness and a better quality of life, but heart training is the *only* training that aids longevity. When the heart last longer, we live longer. Continued training can even raise your resting heart rate, which gives you more energy and makes you feel younger. Training your heart truly is a pathway toward the fountain of youth.

As integral as the heart is to our physical lives, so too is it vitally important to our walk with God:

- "Keep your heart with all diligence, for out of it are the issues of life" (Prov. 4:23).
- "And you shall seek me, and find me, when you shall search for me with all your heart" (Jer. 29:13).
- "For with the heart man believes unto righteousness; and with the mouth, confession is made unto salvation" (Rom. 10:10).

The heart is the place where we first believed, and it's the place Jesus wants to live in. When we become believers, God gives us a new heart. We understand right from wrong—and hopefully we desire right—but there are attitudes of the heart that still need sanctification. "The heart is deceitful above all things, and desperately wicked; who can know it. I the Lord search the heart; I try the reins, even to give every man according to his ways, and according to the fruit of his doings" (Jer. 17:9–10).

The heart is so important that its godly attitudes can invite God's blessings into our lives, and it's ungodly attitudes can actually stop God from blessing us. Remember what the Lord said to the Prophet Samuel at Jessie's house when he anointed David? "For the Lord sees not as a man sees; for man looks on the outward appearance, but the Lord looks on the heart" (1 Sam. 16:7). Our heart is who we are in God's eyes. Samuel thought that Jesse's eldest son was the Lord's anointed, but he was wrong. Now, we can't blame Samuel for making the wrong call because God was the one who started it. There was only one other king chosen at this point, Saul, the tallest and best looking in all of Israel, and God had chosen him. What was Samuel supposed to think? God had even given Saul a new heart as he turned to do the will of God. "And it was so, that when he (King Saul) turned his back to go from Samuel, God gave him another heart" (1 Sam. 10:9). But when Saul's self-seeking, jealous, disobedient, and fearful heart began to rule his life again, God rejected him and chose David because of David's heart.

What we think and value in our hearts makes us who we are. "As he thinks in his heart, so is he" (Prov. 23:7). If we're always thinking of ourselves first, or scheming to get our own way, or getting mad and jealous when others get what we want, or doing whatever we want, oblivious to whether it hurts others or God—that's who we are. On the other hand, if we often think of others' needs, are happy for others when they're blessed, and are careful not to offend others or God, then *that's* who we are. We're not what we say we are; we are what we think and do.

One of the Lord's most effective training routines for our spiritual hearts is patience, especially when we're forced to endure difficulty for a prolonged period of time. What happens in our hearts while the Lord delays can be very revealing. Remember the children of Israel while Moses was delayed on the mountain when receiving the Ten Commandments? They began complaining, made a golden calf, and worshipped it. On one hand we cannot believe they could have acted that way, particularly after experiencing miracle after miracle *and* being fully delivered from Egypt. On the other hand, we sometimes act the same way. When we don't receive the promise of God, we tire of waiting. We either get some attitude in our heart that's not good, or we take matters into our own hands.

We can plainly see this bad attitude when we look at Job's wife. Job's story epitomizes patience, so much so that the New Testament refers to his patience. That's what I call endurance training. But his wife made an interesting comment as things went from bad to worse for their family. She told Job, "Curse God and die."

I think we can call that a bad attitude.

Of course, it's easy for me to say that without having had to endure what she did, but nevertheless, that's what she said. I bet through all of those wonderful years of blessing that she never knew that thought lived in her heart. Much comes out of the heart that we didn't know was in there when we're forced to wait upon the Lord. We battle jealousy when others get the very thing we've been praying for. Or, we struggle with bitterness while feeling that God's not fair to us, or the rejection that he simply doesn't care. It's amazing what can be buried so deeply in our hearts.

We also take matters into our own hands. In fact, the Father of Faith was guilty of this. Abraham began his journey of trusting and following the Lord with a great promise, but his entire life seemed to pass by without that promise ever seeming to come true. When his wife Sarah was in her eighties, she must have laughed every time she said Abraham's name. "Father of a great nation! Ha! He doesn't even have one child, and I will never be getting pregnant."

Years pass and they finally tire of waiting. To force God's hand, they take matters into their own hands. Sarah's handmaiden gives birth to Ishmael, then Abraham sends the boy away. What a sad and devastating event to have happened to that fourteen-year-old boy: to be raised by Abraham for all of those years and circumcised at the age of thirteen, only to be cast away. It's almost unlike God's character to let that happen, but that is what Abraham and Sarah's bright idea led to. Sometimes we create so much trouble for ourselves, and those around us by failing to wait on God. Abraham eventually dies, and who shows up to bury him? That's right: his son Ishmael. Ishmael and Isaac bury their father and both depart to start great nations. It's no wonder that the descendants of Ishmael don't like the Jewish God. It's almost like they were unfairly treated. How heartbreaking it must have been for Ishmael and his mom to walk out into the desert alone with just a loaf of bread and a bottle of water. Thank God that their Father in heaven was watching over them.

Both Abraham and Job's wife gave up in their spiritual endurance training because it can be a heartbreaking process. We've heard many times that the Christian "race" is not a sprint but a marathon. The Boston Marathon is difficult because near its end there's a long incline that seems to never end. Fittingly, it's called "Heartbreak Hill." Many runners think they're nearing the end of the race and give up somewhere on that hill.

That's what it's like in our Christian walk with God sometimes. We're running our race and trusting God, but some things never change and we begin to lose heart. We give up in our heart. It *hurts*. We know God could do something to change things, but he doesn't. We question his concern for us and it can be heartbreaking. Though our spiritual endurance training seems like it's trying our faith to a point we can't endure, it's actually *increasing* our faith. Our desperation causes us to seek God and to know him like never before.

Waiting on God during important life issues can cause us to feel desperate sometimes, and the longer we have to wait, the more desperate we can become. This desperation is supposed to inspire us to seek God with all of our hearts. When things are going great, we think God is happy with us and we give him a thank you every now and then. When things are going bad, we may think he's mad at us and we're not sure how to feel. But what's really happening is that God desires to draw us closer so he can reveal more of himself to us. In God's eyes, this is an intimate relationship that he is working hard to deepen. He has given his all and continues to do so, but we're sometimes so busy with life that we don't have much time to invest in our relationship with him. Being desperate for God to move in our life changes that. We spend hours pouring out our hearts before God, learning about fasting, and begin to seek him with all our hearts.

Scripture says, "You will find me when you search for me with all of your heart." God wants to be found by us. He's like a dad playing hide-and-seek with his young child who can't wait to jump out of hiding and say, "You found me!" God wants us to find him so he can show us himself, help us, and just be with us. Humanity's relationship with God began when God and Adam simply hung out together and enjoyed each other.

God hasn't changed, but we have. God has been waiting for a long time for many of us to come looking for him with all of our hearts, but we have yet to do that. This is the only way we're ever going to truly find him. Days, months, and years may pass and still we're not searching for him, then finally we become desperate and start looking. Being desperate is not a bad place to be in if we know where to look.

God is waiting for us right now. Jesus said, "I stand at the door and knock." If we would just open up that door and start looking we would find him, and everything would change. Look what happened with Job. The Enemy brought destruction upon Job, and his loss forced him to seek God like never before. When it was all said and done, Job makes an interesting comment. "I have heard of thee by the hearing of the ear, but now my eyes see you" (Job 42:5). Job knew about God, but now he knows God personally. Job was forced to seek God, then found him, and then everything changed.

Our goal in waiting on God is not to see our circumstances change because that can be frustrating. Our goal should be to find God, and when we do everything will change. God wants to be found by us and that's what waiting on God and being patient is all about. Moses waited forty years and then saw God in the burning bush, his greatest years still ahead of him. Abraham finally received the promise and gained so much faith in all that waiting that he was able to consider sacrificing Isaac, figuring God would raise him from the dead. That is spiritual endurance for our hearts, because when we find God, we are refreshed. It's like getting our second wind in a long endurance race and being able to continue with vigor and zeal as this verse shows. "But they that wait upon the Lord shall renew their strength; they shall mount up with wings as eagles; they shall run, and not be weary; they shall walk, and not be faint" (Isa. 40:31).

We can't allow ourselves to give up at this point because we're on the edge of a major breakthrough. It's not just in our relationship with God, but it's deep in our heart. This is the place where our hearts are changed forever. The only way to get through these times is to let go of what we're waiting for and to fall into the arms of Jesus. We have to come to the place that Jesus did in the garden of Gethsemane when he said, "Nevertheless not my will, but thy will be done" (Luke 22:42). It's here where our heart changes, we surrender and find God in a whole new way. This is when miracles start happening because now God is in control.

Look at Jesus, the greatest endurance of all-time. He remained on the cross when he could have gotten off at anytime. He surrendered to the Father's will for better or worse. He endured the cross and humanity was changed forever. Endurance training for the heart is patiently waiting for God's will.

It's amazing to think about how foreign a concept such patient endurance is to us today. We're so conditioned to having things right away that we become frustrated at the slightest delay. Slow Internet speeds, rush-hour traffic, and long lines at the stores can very quickly bother us. Whenever we encounter a delay, we see it as a problem. The thought never occurs to us that *we* might be a little too impatient. We humans are a funny bunch, and it can be very easy to satisfy us. We just want what we want, and we want it now. If that happens, we're happy, but if not we can become frustrated or even angry. The Enemy wants to steal our joy and peace, so he magnifies these delays and tries to make God look bad. Is us getting what we want what our relationship with God is all about?

Nehemiah says, "The joy of the Lord is your strength" (Neh. 8:10). Trusting that God still loves us and has a plan for us through long delays gives us such strength of heart and character. It's where the peace that passes understanding is created, and where the faith to move mountains is developed. There's such a confidence that comes with trusting that God is in control, it's where the Christian life comes alive. It's where we stand in the face of adversity, unmoved by the uncertainty swirling around us.

While remodeling a home years ago, I was on a sixty-foot ladder fully extended to the top of the house. If you've never experienced that, it can be a little scary, because a strong gust of wind could knock you off, sending you to a sure death. Suddenly, fifty crows started flying around me, screeching like they were being tortured. I'd never heard anything like that in my life. I thought I was surely going to meet my Maker soon. Hitchcock's *The Birds* began playing in my mind. I held on to the peak of the house with both hands, just waiting for this murder of crows to start pecking me to death and knock me off the ladder.

And that's when I saw what the commotion was all about: about ten feet away from me, a huge bird of prey had landed on the chimney. He was awesome. None of the crows dared to get close to him because they knew it would mean *their* certain death. At first I thought, "Great, now *this* huge bird is going to knock me off the ladder and kill me."

But after a while I noticed something. This bird didn't seem bothered by the situation. It was as if he couldn't even hear or see those crazy crows all around him. He was just relaxing, taking it easy, and checking me out. He stayed there for the longest time, and as I gazed upon him the words "quiet confidence" came to me.

That's what God wants to do with us. He wants to give us a quiet confidence in knowing that everything is going to be OK because he is in control, and to not hear all of the Enemy's threats working through our fears and apprehensions. God wants to give us joy, peace, and confidence as we're waiting for him to show up, and trusting God through these long delays is his training routine. God wants to come through for us like the knight in shining armor that he is.

So next time you find yourself forced to believe and wait on God, don't run from the situation. Don't let those bad attitudes creep in, and don't take matters into your own hands. Don't fight with those around you, and don't worry. Just be still and know that he is God. Trust in God's character and trust in God's Word. "Thus says the Lord to you; do not be afraid nor dismayed . . . for the battle is not yours, but God's" (2 Chron. 20:15).

CHAPTER 5

FLEXIBILITY TRAINING: FOLLOWING GOD

Stretching is one of the most underestimated needs in fitness. Training muscles makes them tight, but stretching muscles lengthens them and releases the tightness. Stretching also protects us from injury, because the better our flexibility is, the less likely we are to tear muscles and stress tendons. It's amazing how many people live with chronic lower back pain, and in many cases lower back and hamstring stretching would cure their pain. Stretching has great benefits.

Flexibility is not something we can force. When we build muscles, we force heavy weights on ourselves. When we do cardio, we force our hearts to beat faster. When we're stretching, there's no forcing at all. We're relaxing, releasing, and allowing the process to happen. Like a knee-jerk reaction, our body automatically stops stretching at a certain point to help avoid injury. We can bend to a certain point and that's it, but if we hold that point and begin to relax and breathe deeply, our body shifts gears and allows us to stretch much deeper. It's like our body trusts us now and then releases its grip on the muscles. Breathing deeply and not being in a hurry are key.

It's amazing how young and energetic you may feel as you continue with flexibility training. I've seen countless people who move around like they're one hundred years old, but after months of this kind of training, they feel like teenagers. So, if you're a little stiff in the morning, try stretching. It will do wonders for you.

Flexibility is also important in our walk with God. There were those in the Old Testament, who were a little stiff, and it had everything to do with being led by God "And the Lord said unto Moses, I have seen this people, and behold, it is a stiff-necked people" (Ex. 32:9). God is about to give them the Ten Commandments and lead them to the Promised Land, but they said, "We want to go back to Egypt." Nearly every time God calls them stiff-necked, rebellious, and stubborn, he's trying to lead them somewhere and they refuse. I love how descriptive the word "stiff-necked" is, as if God is trying to turn our head in a certain direction but we won't let him. God must be thinking to himself, "I'm trying to turn this head so they can see my will, but that darn neck won't let go. That's one stiff neck." Of course he could force it to bend, but that would break our neck and kill us. So when it comes to being led by God, being flexible can make all the difference.

When we think of stubbornness, one animal immediately comes to mind: the donkey. If you try to get them to go in one direction, they refuse. They will sit down on their butts if they have to, but they're not going to obey. People can be just like that, hence the phrase "stubborn as a mule."

But that's not who we are as God's people. We're sheep. "The sheep hear my voice, and follow me" (John 10:27). Jesus is the Good Shepherd who loves us. He wants to bring us to that place of green grass and safe pastures. He knows where they are, and if we just follow him the Lord will lead us there. When we refuse to go, we're really hurting ourselves and keeping ourselves from the beautiful destiny God has prepared for us.

One reason we act this way is because we think we know better. We live in this real world and self-preservation tends to take authority over everything else. Remember the ten spies' report in the Promised Land? They essentially said, "They're big and we're little, and we'll die if we go in." So they refused God's direction and became rebellious.

The truth is that all who refused to go in did die in the desert, and all who wanted to go in lived, namely Joshua and Caleb. Sometimes the direction God calls us to go in might not make sense, but nevertheless it's the path to blessing and destiny. We have to be careful— and not so set in our ways—that we miss out when God opens a door for us to walk through. We have to be flexible enough that at a moment's notice we can be turned without worrying about the outcome of our quick decision.

We see this flexible attitude very clearly during the apostle Paul's missionary journeys. As a door in one area would close, it would send him in another direction to where God wanted him to go next. He didn't stubbornly fight and try to force himself into those places, but instead he accepted God's will and began to look for new opportunities to open up—and they always did. He trusted that God was leading him, and he knew that closed doors were often God's way of revealing his future plans for Paul.

Paul seemed to always make the right decision while following God's direction, but it can be the hardest thing to do. The Enemy usually attacks us and tries to make it difficult for us to do God's will, so it can be hard to tell whether it's God closing a door or the Enemy trying to discourage us. The plain truth is that it is very difficult at times to know what to do. What God is trying to develop in us is a sensitivity to everything happening around us: the people we meet, their needs, and the resistance we encounter. God is trying to lead us quite often by the circumstances of life.

Years ago my friend needed money for rent. I had not been working for a while due to the economy, so I couldn't really afford to help. As I dropped her off at her apartment, I noticed it was in a little disrepair. I thought to myself, "I'll call her landlord and offer to do a little work to pay her rent." I wasn't working anyway. Not only did he pay me twice as much as she needed in return for just a few days of my work, but I went on to work for him for the next twelve months, renovating all of his properties. I was sensitive to God, just trying to be a blessing, and the Holy Spirit directed me. I'd like to say that I notice those opportunities all the time, but I don't. It could have been so easy for me to miss that, and I wonder how much of that we miss every day.

God wants to lead us. In other words, God wants us to follow him. We see this in the way Jesus called his disciples. "Follow me," he said, and that's exactly what they did. They learned all about the Kingdom of God and how God wanted to use them by following Jesus and learning how he did things. It was all about the relationship. When we allow God to turn our heads in a direction, and we trust him enough to start walking that way by releasing our control and allowing God's will to happen, we will learn everything we need to know.

Look at King David in the cave of Adullam. "And everyone that was in distress, and everyone that was in debt . . . gathered themselves unto him; and he became captain over them" (1 Sam. 22:2). David was hiding from King Saul, and these men came to him and became his army. They became some of the greatest men in the Bible because they spent time with David and learned from him. These men were with David when God had King Saul come into the very cave in which they were hiding. The men essentially said, "Look! God brought Saul here so we can kill him," but David knew better. Still, David cut off a piece of his garment so Saul would know that he could have killed him. Even that act grieved David. His men were there when an opportunity to take Saul's life happened again. God put a heavy sleep on Saul's men so that David's men could go in and take Saul's belongings. Again, David wouldn't lift a hand against the Lord's anointed. These men watched David serve God, and they followed him and his example and likewise became great.

Much of being directed by God is for us to get to know him and learn from him, but some of us just can't do that. We can't just let go and trust God because there's no guarantee. Look at the story of the rich young ruler. "Then Jesus beholding him, loved him and said, 'There's one thing that you lack: go sell all your possessions and give them to the poor and follow me'" (Matt. 19:21). Jesus gave this man the same invitation he did the other twelve disciples. He simply said, "Follow me." This Scripture says that Jesus loved him, so this was a very special person. The Lord was trying to help him. The one thing he lacked was trust, because we all know we can trust in money or we can trust in God. This is what God is trying to teach us as we follow him into situations that don't make sense: we can trust him.

> The young man went away sorrowful. Following Jesus didn't make sense to him and he had too much to lose. Jesus could have been calling him to replace Judas. He might have traveled with Paul on his missionary journeys, or his shadow could have healed people like Peter's shadow once did. We'll never know because the rich young ruler wasn't willing to let go and trust God.

When God calls us to do something and we refuse, it's usually because we think we know what's going to happen. The only thing wrong with that is that we fail to leave room for the supernatural. When it comes to the supernatural, we don't know what we don't know, and unless we trust God and follow his will; we'll never know what could have actually happened.

Peter believed the Lord called him out of the boat to walk on water, and he did so. David believed God wanted him to fight Goliath, and he did so. Caleb said he was well able to take the land if the Lord be with him, and he did so. Joshua believed God wanted them to cross the Jordan on dry ground, and they did so. Moses believed God wanted him to hold up the staff so the Red Sea would part, and he did so.

Unless we're willing to step out and risk, we might never see the power of God demonstrated through our lives. The truth is, we don't know what's going to happen—we only think we do. We're human people trying to understand the spiritual while God is trying to make us into spiritual people inside a human body. The understanding that we have to come to is that God is the one trying to accomplish this, and just like stretching, our job is to give in, relax, and trust.

One of the best examples of this comes from the book of Jeremiah. "As the clay is in the potters hand, so are you in mine" (Jer. 18:6). God says, "I want you to be like clay in my hands so I can mold you into whatever I want." God wants us to be flexible enough to go with whatever he might want to do, but oftentimes we fight that. We say we don't want to be like that, we fight God's molding, and we refuse to follow or go along with his plan. Isaiah pronounces judgment upon those that do this: "Woe unto him that strives with his Maker! . . . Shall the clay say to him that formed it, 'Why make this?'" (Isa. 45:9). The apostle Paul is trying to reason with us in this verse. "Hath not the potter power over the clay, of the same lump to make one vessel unto honor, and another unto dishonor?" (Rom. 9:21). Paul is effectively saying, "How can you say why to God? He's God. He breathed life into us. We are his creation. God's desire is to shape our way of thinking and acting into what he's planned from the beginning, and allowing him to lead us helps to accomplish that."

Remember in Acts 10 when God led Peter to go preach to the Gentiles in Caesarea? The night before, Peter had a dream about eating unclean food, but he still wasn't getting the message God intended for him. Then, before he's done preaching, the Holy Spirit falls on every Gentile. Suddenly, the church's theology changes. Gentiles can now become believers. God showed them that as they simply followed him. The reason God didn't let Peter finish his sermon is because when he was done, Peter would have said, "But this is only for the Jews, not you unclean Gentiles." I'm mostly kidding. I don't know that for sure. But God wasn't taking any chances. You never know with Peter, and you never know with us. Remember in Acts 15 when Paul said it was too much for Gentile converts to have to get circumcised? God showed that to Paul through his journeys, and again the church's theology radically changed. (I'm sure all of the Gentile converts were glad to hear that!)

God wants us to be sensitive to what he is doing and go with it. It's like dancing: the man leads and the woman follows. It can be hard for us men to understand this because we lead. Women who dance can often understand this better because they follow. Take West Coast swing dancing for instance. The woman follows every move the man makes. It's such a wonderful dance. The woman goes where the man leads her, and the man tries to display the woman in all her beauty to all that are watching. If we are the brides of Christ, he is the man in this dance of life.

Never is this point more evident than in the life of Paul the apostle. He learns right from the beginning to be led by God. God blinds him, so he needs someone to lead him. For three days he has to be led to the bathroom and to the kitchen table, and they had to put a fork in his hand. I'm sure he had a hard time. Paul was realizing just how blind he was to the things of God, and how desperately he needed help. It would do us well as Christians to realize that we too are blind to some of the things of God and become desperate for him to lead us.

Saul gets blinded and is then led to Damascus. His eyes are opened and he's renamed Paul. He then begins preaching Christ and goes wherever God tells him to go. Paul becomes the greatest missionary the world has ever seen, and none of it made any sense. He should have been sent to Israel. No one could connect the dots and declare Christ to be the Messiah like Paul. He learned it all and he knew it all. His first sermon in Damascus makes it so undeniably obvious that Jesus is the Christ that they wanted to kill him. So what does God do? He sends him to the Gentiles. Are you kidding me? And who ends up going to

Israel but Peter, an unlearned fisherman? Don't try to figure it out because your brain will short-circuit. That's how we have to look at being led by God. Don't try to figure it out. It might not make sense now, but it will later.

If you ever want to see a drill sergeant turn red and come unglued, just ask, "Why?" when he tells you to do something. As former military, I know the answer: he'll get in your face and scream at you to try and drum into you the importance of just following orders. He knows that if you ask why in wartime, you'll get killed. Doing what he says right when he says it keeps you alive. I don't mean to be overly dramatic, but it's like that for us. We're in God's army, and the best thing we can do when God says go is to go.

When you see a couple that has been dancing together for years, they move as one. The woman instinctively knows where the man will lead her next. God wants us to be flexible with our plans and allow him to direct us so we can get to know him and what he wants to do next. It's all about the relationship and trusting that Father knows best.

CHAPTER 6

NUTRITION: GOD'S HEART

Nutrition plays a major role in fitness. A person sculpted like a Greek god and one who's overweight can have the same training routine, yet their bodies differ so drastically because of what they put in their mouths. What's even more amazing is that an overweight person can change the way they eat and *become* that perfect physique.

The human body is an amazing machine that requires fuel, and water is essential. When we drink lots of water our body is happy. Water aids every process. We desire protein to replenish muscles, and some carbohydrates and vegetables help the body function properly. It's a very simple equation: when we give our bodies proper nourishment, they'll run like a brand new sports car.

Being overweight can be easy to fix: just eat meals that are high in protein and low in carbs. The body needs carbs for fuel, so if we stop providing carbs the body has to dig into its stored fat reserves. Then, the weight just falls off. We turn our bodies into fat-burning machines.

One reason many of us are out of shape is that we indulge our appetites (or should I say overindulge?). We look at desserts and think of how yummy they are and we indulge. We think of processed fast foods and can't wait to dig in. Rich restaurant foods, and all that bread that turns to glucose, tends to expand our waistlines. Ice cream, cake, candy, chips, and soda all seem irresistible. The body is held prisoner to its appetite. Even though such overindulgence leads to high blood pressure, diabetes, and eventually obesity, we don't care. We can't live without our junk food. Unhealthy nutrition causes an unhealthy body in one way or another.

When it comes to the spiritual world and nutrition, we usually think about what we indulge in. Good spiritual nutrition is reading the Bible, praying, and similar spiritual disciplines. There are many Scriptures that compare those very important aspects of our Christian walk to what nourishes us, and we'll get to those shortly. But in the story of the woman at the well in John 4:7, Jesus declared that there was something else that was actually food to him.

Though a woman and a Samaritan, someone of little regard then, Jesus takes time and talks with this woman at the well. He reveals her innermost secrets, talks of the spiritual world, and then reveals that he is the Christ. And all this for a person who was considered nothing! The disciples marveled that he even spoke to her. When she left to tell the townspeople, the Lord said to the disciples, "I have meat to eat that you know not of" (John 4:32). Jesus explains, "My meat is to do the will of him that sent me, and to finish his work. Say not, there are yet four months, and then comes the harvest? Behold, I say unto you, lift up your eyes, and look on the fields; for they are white already to harvest" (John 4: 34–35).

Jesus is saying that sharing the gospel and seeing people come to salvation is what feeds his soul. This is healthy nutrition in the spiritual world. The whole city comes out and a two-day revival begins. Let's look at this from the eyes of Jesus. In Chapter 1, he rounds up the disciples. In Chapter 2, he reluctantly turns water into wine that his mother pushes on him. In Chapter 3, Jesus wrestles with Nicodemus about issues like being born again. Then in Chapter 4, Jesus says he has to go through Samaria. (I guess he was getting a little hungry.) Jesus poured out everything he had before this woman, and she then tells everyone about her encounter. He tries to explain to the disciples that this is his food, but they don't get it. They start talking to each other about who brought him food. When the whole town came out to him I bet he started salivating. He probably pointed to the gathering crowd and said to the disciples, "Behold, lift up your eyes and look; the fields are white ready to harvest" (John 4:35). In other words, "Let's eat."

The Lord was trying to show the disciples what a big deal this was. Harvest time came once a year, and you had to gather enough food to sustain you until the next harvest. The Scriptures say that all of heaven rejoices over one soul who receives the Lord, which sounds like a big deal. Jesus is talking about the harvesting of souls, and this is what feeds the Lord. It's not only people coming to the Lord that feeds the soul, but it is when we're doing what God has called us to do. Remember, Jesus says, "My meat is to do the will of him that sent me."

When people are involved in the life and the work of the Lord, it feeds God and he becomes satisfied:

- When we share testimonies or receive salvation.
- When we worship the Lord and it goes beyond just speaking words, and somehow our hearts and our love begins to pour out.
- When we pray for each other, encourage each other, and are concerned for each other.
- When we spend time with the Lord in prayer, in the Word, and in fasting.
- When we are involved in church and ministry
- When we reach out to the less fortunate.

These things feed the Lord and bring him satisfaction. God is Spirit and God is love. God is a big, beautiful, forgiving, loving, spiritual heart. All of these things feed his Spirit and heart and bring him satisfaction, and it's the same for us. This is what the Lord was trying to show the disciples.

When we think of food in our human bodies, we think of it going to our stomach and us becoming full. I loved when my mom made lasagna. I would come into the house and smell that aroma, then put it in my mouth and taste that flavor, and then eat so much that my belly would be busting. My stomach was truly satisfied. When it comes to spiritual food, it touches our spirits, encourages our minds, and satisfies our hearts. In the Sermon on the Mount, the Lord said, "Blessed are those that hunger and thirst after righteousness for they shall be filled" (Matt. 5:6). Jesus is saying that they will be totally satisfied. One reason some people are not satisfied with the Christian life is because they're missing this key ingredient to spiritual nutrition. There is a side to Christianity that feeds our spirit.

All that feeds the Lord is relational. Whether it's us to God or us to others, or even us to ourselves, seeking spiritual sustenance involves people. God is relational to the core, and he's made us the same way. There is a satisfaction that comes to our hearts and spirits as we seek God and desire to be a blessing to people. In our current world, money, position, and power are big deals, and people can become satisfied to some extent by attaining them. But in the spiritual side of life, *people* are the big deal!

Somewhere in our walk with God, we're going to have to come to grips with the importance of people. God's greatest treasure is people. In the parable of the sheep and goats, Jesus said, "You clothed me and fed me." They replied, "When?" He said, "When you did it to the least, you did it to me." Jesus also said, "But who shall offend one of these little ones . . . it were better for him that a millstone were hanged about his neck, and that he were drowned in the depth of the sea" (Matt. 18:6). It's like a father saying, "If you mess with one of my kids, you're going to wish you were dead when I get a hold of you."

People are the Lord's precious treasure and he loves them. The Lord came to seek and save those who are lost like some of us—all of us—were. The last words of Jesus were, "Go into all the world and preach the gospel to every creature" (Matt. 28:19). This is supposed to be our food we can't live without: sharing the gospel and stirring our faith again, praying with others for salvation and remembering what salvation was like for us.

I marvel when I see a precious soul-winner. Their eyes seem to sparkle when sharing the Lord. You can't offend them because they just love you like Jesus does. The Bible says they're going to shine like the firmament in heaven. We're going to know them a mile away because of their brightness and because of the crowd gathered around them, that is, everyone who's in heaven because of their witness.

But for some reason, many are not moved by this. Some say that it's just not my thing. They don't need the bother or the time and investment it takes. They believe there's really nothing in it for them. We grew up in a world that teaches us to use and manipulate people to get what we want, and we become jaded by scam artists who would take advantage of us, so we don't trust. People hurt others with slander and name-calling. They lie, steal, and cheat to get ahead and say, "It's nothing personal. It's just business." Well, it is personal, and when they stand before God they're going to get the business.

We can't allow the way of the world to poison us. God has called us to go into the world and shine his love and to bring hope. The world is really starving for affection, and God's desire is for us to feed them with his love. Just like good nutrition feeds our muscles and makes us physically strong, this is the kind of food that makes us strong in the Spirit. There is a wonderful satisfaction that comes with doing the will of God and pouring out our lives into others.

Here's another glimpse into spiritual food: "It's not what goes in the mouth that defiles a person; it's what comes out" (Mark 7:15). Jesus then lists hurting people, evil thoughts, adultery, murder, theft, deceit, an evil eye, and blasphemy. When we treat people badly, we distance ourselves from God. We can't hurt God more than when we hurt others, and he makes this one point the clearest in the whole Bible. Not only do we distance ourselves from God, but we cross a line and become a tool that the Enemy uses to hurt God's creation and in so doing hurt God.

The Lord wants beautiful and encouraging words to come out of our mouths. He wants what we say to drip with faith, hope, and love, covered in grace, and laced with direction and correction. God wants his Spirit to come out of our mouths so that its hearers can be helped. The way that happens is by understanding the importance of people and cultivating God's Spirit in our hearts, because it's out of the abundance of the heart that the mouth speaks.

So there is something about loving people and sharing the gospel that nourishes us. Perhaps it's being so close to the heart of God that the Lord infuses us with something. Or maybe the relationship we create feeds us in some way, or the love of God that's being enlarged in us is filling some need we have. Whatever it is, one thing is for sure: loving others is just as important for us as it is for the people we reach out to. It is the spiritual food God wants us to eat so we can become spiritually big and strong.

The Bible also refers to itself as food for us to eat, or should I say read. As we read, understand, and do God's Word, we are fed and made stronger. We are encouraged not to just live on earthly sustenance for our physical bodies, but to feed our spirits. "Man does not live by bread alone, but by every word that proceeds out of the mouth of God" (Deut. 8:3). God is saying that just like our bodies need food to survive, so do our spirits, and the words of God are what feed us. Just like we have an appetite for food we love to eat, God's Word should affect us the same way. "How sweet are your words to my taste, yes, sweeter than honey"(Ps. 119:103). It sounds more like dessert in that verse, but it's food all the same, and we should long for it and desire it.

When we first become believers, we usually don't know much about God. It's through reading, studying, and meditating on God's Word that we come to know what God is like and what the Christian life is all about. We are considered as babes or infants. "As newborn babes, desire the sincere milk of the word" (1 Peter 2:2). What a great example. Everything a newborn baby needs to grow to be big and strong is contained in the breast milk. God is saying that as we read the word, it has that same effect on us: we are being fed. God's Word has everything we need. It's such a beautiful thing to see a newborn latch on to the mother's nipple for the first time and to realize that they're being fed. What a miracle. It's like when a new believer reads something in the Bible that relates to exactly what they're going through and they grow stronger and closer to the Lord as a result of it. What a miracle.

One of the names of Jesus is "El Shaddai," the many-breasted one, a picture of nourishing and comforting many with himself. As wonderful a picture as that is, God's desire for us is that we eventually move from being breastfed to eating for ourselves. I knew a woman that continued to breastfeed until her son was over four years old, and it didn't seem to have quite the same sense of awe. Let's keep that picture in mind as we read this next Scripture. "For the time you ought to be teachers, you have need that one teaches you again . . . and are become such as need of milk, and not of strong meat. For everyone that uses milk is unskillful in the word . . . for he is a babe" (Heb. 5:12–13). God is saying that there should come a time in our Christian walk when we grow up and start eating meat. He doesn't want us to drink breast milk our entire life.

Yes, the first principles never grow old. They are just as amazing now as they were when we first believed—Jesus dying on the cross for us, forgiving all of our sins by grace, and becoming heaven bound for all eternity. The apostle Paul was brilliant and professed to know nothing but Christ and him crucified. As amazing and life-changing as those principles are, if that is as far as our Christian experience goes we are not maturing in our personal lives. Those principles are our foundation and designed to be built upon, but I'll talk more about that in my next book. God wants us to grow up and live this life, and we learn to do that through the word. Now, of course the Lord is always there to comfort us and nourish us, and I'm not trying to make light of that. As an older believer, there are many times that I am grateful that Jesus is still "the many-breasted one" and is always there for me. The point that the Scripture is making is that we should be maturing, and the Scriptures instruct us on how that's done.

God's Word has everything we need. It is a veritable smorgasbord. It has everything contained in it to bring us from infancy to full maturity. The Bible begins by showing us how to live. God's Word instructs us and corrects us. "All scripture is given by inspiration of God, and is profitable for doctrine, for reproof, for correction, for instruction in righteousness" (2 Tim. 3:16). The Bible is not just a book written by man, but the words contained in it were given by the inspiration of God. God wrote this book! They are not just nice thoughts to consider, but they are the substance upon which we should be building our life. God created man and then he wrote the owner's manual. When we purchase a new car, it comes with an owner's manual. The designer of the car wrote it to instruct us on the care of it, and it's the same for us. The Bible is the owner's manual for our lives.

When we don't know God's Word or fail to follow its guidance, we're prone to making mistakes and missing out on what is available to us. "You do err, not knowing the scriptures, nor the power of God" (Matt. 22:29). The limitless power of God is available to us as Christians, but if we never read of all his promises, or his way of releasing it, we may never experience it. It's like driving a Ferrari sports car and never shifting out of first gear because we've never learned about second gear. Even though we have amazing horsepower at our fingertips, it's to no avail. The car was built for speed and handling, but we'll never experience it until we learn to shift gears. It's through the reading and understanding of God's Word that we're enlightened and realize how everything works. Feeding on the Word of God teaches us how to shift gears into maturity and discover the power of God in our lives. There's a lot more power under the hood of that old Bible than we give it credit for, and our Father in heaven wants us to experience it.

God's Word also created everything. "The worlds were framed by the word of God, so that things which are seen were not made of things which do appear" (Heb. 11:3). The universe and all of life were spoken into existence. God spoke it and his words made it happen. God's Word is powerful. "The word of God is quick, and powerful, and sharper than a two-edged sword" (Heb. 4:12). God wants to teach us how to wield this powerful sword so that every word spoken in it comes alive in our lives. God said it, I believe it, and that settles it, so why don't you crack your Bible open and take a bite?

You could be transformed overnight.

CHAPTER 7

THE BODY: THE CHURCH

The human body is the most amazing creation that has ever come into existence. All this talk about fitness only scratches the surface. The heart beats, the lungs breathe, and the body moves—what a miracle. Then there are the senses: the eyes see and focus, the ears hear, the nose smells, fingers and toes touch and feel, and our tongues taste. Then there are the emotions: we feel happy, sad, mad, and a million other feelings. Then there's the brain, the big daddy of them all. It's the central computer that controls everything by interpreting visuals, discerning aromas, questioning tastes, and understanding noises. It blows my mind to think about the mind. It commands the entire body to move, it calculates and comes to decisions, and it creates and invents. Everything we see around us started as a thought in a mind, except nature, and we even try to cultivate and control that. God made a human body, placed it on planet Earth, and things started happening.

Sadly, not all humans function properly. Some minds don't work, some emotions are damaged, and some senses and bodily functions are broken. Those who are forced to endure such limitations on a daily basis are often more challenged in life than those whose bodies work the way they were intended to. It's inspiring to watch the Special Olympics or witness someone who has overcome their situation and desires to excel nevertheless. What a precious spirit of victory. Their strength of heart humbles me whenever I'm with them! I say all that to say there's much going on inside these bodies God gave each of us.

God also has a body on planet Earth. "For as we have many members in one body . . . so we, being many, are one body in Christ, and every one members one of another" (Rom. 12:4–5). We are one body in Christ. Together we are the physical body of Jesus. The church is not supposed to be about God, it's supposed to be the place he manifests himself. God's great love and compassion should be seen in the interaction of its members, to the point that God becomes visible. Desiring to pray for each other's needs, and experiencing those prayers being answered, and needs being met. Church members ought to be able to enter church depressed and despondent and leave joyful and hopeful, without even being able to explain why. Some may even experience prayer for a physical miracle and see it happen instantly or in due time. The church is God's body, and whenever we gather he is there.

Remember when Solomon finished building God's house and everyone came together and opened up the ark? "And it came to pass, when the priests came out of the holy place, that the cloud filled the house of the Lord. So that the priest could not stand to minister because of the cloud: for the glory of the Lord had filled the house of the Lord" (1 Kings 8:10–11). That's what I call a good church service. God wants to show himself to the world, and he wants to do it through his body.

This event bears a striking resemblance to another group that gathered together waiting for God to show up at Pentecost. "They were all in one accord, and in one place. And suddenly there came a sound from heaven as of a rushing mighty wind . . . and there appeared unto them cloven tongues as of fire . . . and they were all filled with the Holy Ghost" (Acts 2:1–4). That must have been another great church service. The Lord's body was in one place and in one accord and the Lord showed up. Of course, the key is being in one accord, because if half of a body wants to go one way and half wants to go another, that body won't be going very far or get much accomplished. The Bible says that a double-minded person is unstable in all his ways; so is a double-minded church. Consequently, when it comes to being part of God's body, unity plays a major role: "Endeavoring to keep the unity of the Spirit, in the bond of peace" (Eph. 4:3).

It's our job as part of the body to focus on unity. One way to accomplish that is to focus on what we have in common, to consider what draws us together rather than what divides. So many times we focus on those insignificant things that divide and not on those major things we have in common, like spending eternity together, sharing in the same great commission, and having the same Father in heaven. We would rather not have anything to do with each other because of social differences or spiritual disagreements, like when the rapture is going to happen. Many times we only want to have unity with those that look, think, and act like us, but God wants us to have unity with *all* of our church body. On the danger of being divided, Jesus said, "Every kingdom divided against itself is brought to desolation, and a house divided against itself falls" (Luke 11:17). Jesus wasn't just saying that as another great comeback to the Pharisee's ridiculous comments. It's a spiritual truth that also applies to the church.

Lacking suspicion also helps with promoting unity. It is so easy to be suspicious of others. We automatically think, "What does this person want?" We want to judge motives and critique actions like we're perfect, when of course we're not. God wants us to love our brothers and sisters and give them the benefit of the doubt. God wants us to have the mindset of this Scripture: "Whatsoever things are true . . . honest . . . just . . . pure . . . lovely . . . of good report . . . if there be any virtue . . . any praise, think on these things" (Phil. 4:8). Whatever happened to being innocent until proven guilty? We are brothers and sisters. We are not in competition with each other, and we don't need to have the attention as the Lord makes clear in these two Scriptures: "Be ye all of one mind, have compassion one for another, love as brethren, be pitiful, be courteous" (1 Peter 3:8). "Let nothing be done through strife or vainglory; but in loneliness of mind let each esteem others better than themselves" (Phil. 2:3). God should be the one getting the attention. We should be glad when our brothers and sisters excel, even if they pass right by us. This is what a body is like. My stomach loves my mouth, especially when it's eating something yummy. My back loves my hand when it's scratching an itchy spot. My lungs love how my nose inhales oxygen.

If people could only see the trouble they cause and the pain they inflict when they try to bring in strife and cause discord. "He that passes by and meddles with strife belonging not to him, is like one that takes a dog by the ears" (Prov. 26:17). What a great illustration. I love the Lord's humor. Imagine a dog sitting down, happily minding its own business, and then for no reason someone comes by and grabs its ears. I feel bad for the poor dog; it's like animal abuse. Of course, we know that sometimes the person grabbing the ears gets bit. God's body being in unity is so important we need to contend for it.

We read in 1 Corinthians 12:15–27 how silly it is to think we don't need each other. "Can the eye say to the hand I have no need for you?" We can all agree that's a silly statement, because we need our hands just like we need our eyes. But in this real world we really don't need each other. We have our lives and our families. We really don't need the people at the church we attend. People can be so much work, in listening to what they have to say that doesn't interest us in the least and in all those favors people need. Yes, we can definitely do without the people at church, but that's the human side of life, not the spiritual. The Bible is very clear about our need for each other: "For where two or three are gathered together in my name, there am I in the midst" (Matt. 18:20). God is drawn to our coming together. The illustration that comes to me is that God is steel, and our coming together is like a magnet. When we come together in his name, the magnet gets stronger. There is an unseen force drawing God to us when we gather, and that's exactly the way he designed it. We are spiritually stronger when we unite. The Scriptures are full of examples. There's Queen Esther, who is maybe a little hesitant to do what she should, so Mordecai encourages her: "Who knows whether you have come to the Kingdom for such a time as this" (Esther 4:14). Then Queen Esther replies along the lines of, "Everyone start fasting, I'm going in! It's against the law, so if I die, I die!" Wow, what a woman. Two people came together and God moved. They needed each other.

Then there's Ruth, an amazing woman of God. Truly revealing the heart of Jesus, she tells Naomi, "I'll never leave you." Then, by the hand of God and Naomi's advice, Ruth becomes part of the lineage of Christ (Ruth 3:3–4). I'll paraphrase Naomi's advice: "Ruth, honey, take a shower, put some perfume on and a nice little outfit, go to the party, and keep an eye on Boaz. When he's done partying and passes out, go lay beside him." Naomi helped Ruth show Boaz her affection. The two women saw God's hand moving and went with it. They needed each other.

Then there's the time Jesus sent the seventy out two-by-two and they returned rejoicing, "Saying 'Lord, even the devils are subject to us in your name.' And the Lord said: 'I beheld Satan as lightning fall from Heaven'" (Luke 10:17–18). They were not sent out one-by-one because they needed each other. Jesus knew that it multiplied their authority in the spiritual world because God was in their midst.

My personal favorite is the dynamic duo of Jonathan and David. Jonathan was every bit as anointed and spiritually powerful as David. While David was still a young shepherd boy, Jonathan slew hundreds of valiant Philistines at one time with only his armor-bearer following. He was in line to be the next king and probably learned from the prophet Samuel. God was with him, and when he saw David kill Goliath, Jonathan must have thought to himself, "I love this guy—he reminds me a lot of myself." Jonathan decided that if God wanted David to be King instead of himself, then so be it. Jonathan wasn't filled with jealousy like his father was, but he loved David and wanted to help any way that he could. They were two of the most valiant and fearless men to ever grace the pages of our sacred book. David said that the love he had for Jonathan surpassed that of a woman. Jonathan loved David as his own soul. If we can get to this place as Christians, no Enemy in hell could stop us. God is trying to show us that we need each other, even if we think we don't. "Two are better than one . . . for if they fall, the one will lift up his fellow, but woe to him that is alone when he falls" (Ecc. 4:9–10).

If the Lord could open our eyes for a second, we could see a lot more going on than that, as we'll try to see in the following Scripture. "And let us consider one another to provoke unto love and good works: Not forsaking the assembling of ourselves together" (Heb. 10:24–25). God's body is the *ecclesia*, the "called out to gather." That's our name, that's who we are, and that's what we do. God forces us to congregate so we are forced to consider each other. The needs that we personally become aware of as we come together are supposed to provoke us to act in love through good works, which simply means attempting to meet those very needs.

The wonderful thing about attempting to meet the needs we personally see is that we begin to see who we are in Christ. We begin to find our gifting and anointing, and this church thing starts getting exciting as we see God direct us and move through us. It's through these people at church who we can definitely do without that we become everything God has destined us to be. We need each other more than we think. Our Scripture says, "not forsaking the assembling of ourselves together." I love that God uses descriptive words to let us know exactly how he feels. The word "forsaking" shows how dear our unity is to his heart, like a child that's been forsaken.

When we don't show up, or when we are not moved enough to act upon a need we notice and are able to respond to, something is being neglected. It's like a human body that is damaged and can't function the way it was designed to. God wants his body to be whole. Our example should be the church in the book of Acts. "And all that believed were together, and had all things common. And sold their possessions and goods, and parted them to all men, as every man had need" (Acts 2:44–46). The body was taking care of itself.

I love walking into a church right before service and seeing lots of small groups huddled up where people are praying for each other, empathizing with each other, meeting each other's needs, and encouraging one another. A week of battling is over and we come to receive nourishment and healing to go on. Church then feels like a living organism, and that's just what it is: God's body alive and well, all its parts working together, realizing how important they are to each other and how much they truly need each other, a body in love with itself and in love with God.

One of the funniest things to do is to ask ten different people what the church service was about. You'll get ten different answers. Why? Because we're all different parts of the body. We see things differently. God knows that we're different and he specifically brought us together to help his body. "And he gave some apostles . . . prophets . . . pastors and teachers for the perfecting of the saints, for the work of the ministry, for the edifying of the body" (Eph. 4:11-12).

I don't have an agenda to push church. How many people have been hurt by churches? What a crime. The hospital that's supposed to make us well can sometimes kill us. Can we imagine anything that could break God's heart more than that? But God does say that we are his body, that he wants to move through us, and that he wants us to come together so he can show his power and glory. Not only does this concept apply to us individually concerning the church we attend, but to all churches in the body of Christ. Let's face it: churches are different. They look at their differences and often don't want anything to do with each other. This definitely takes place across denominational lines, but even occurs within denominational borders. Of course, I understand the leadership feeling responsible for the sheep God has entrusted to them. They seek to protect them from things that could hurt them, like children, but at some point we are going to have to trust God and embrace each other.

If we could just see things from God's perspective, maybe our attitude would change. When God looks at all of the different churches, he sees his children. They're all going to be living together for eternity with him, so what's going on down here can be described as sibling rivalry. Each church thinks they're the best, but God is saying, "You're all the best. You're my kids."

Different churches exist because they all meet different needs in the world. Just like one person can't meet every need in a congregation, one church or denomination can't meet every need in the world. Just like people see things differently and have different giftings to find their place in the body, churches do too.

Some churches are all about evangelism. They are always in the community and on the streets sharing the Gospel. These churches don't usually have big bank accounts, but they have huge hearts and are fearless. They are being Jesus to the lost.

Then there are the big churches that are focused on getting their congregation to form smaller groups for fellowship and ministry. They have huge bank accounts and are able to help those less fortunate. They are being Jesus to the poor, and of course impacting their community and much more.

Then there are those churches that are focused on nations overseas. They're all about sending out missionaries, supporting them, and sending teams to help. They are being Jesus to the world.

God made people different to meet different needs, and he made churches different for the same reason. We are all one body. So when we look at other churches in

God's body, we should have the same understanding we do of our local body: to strive for unity, to focus on what we have in common, and to find our place in God's grand plan. If we do so, I think we will bring a big smile to the head of this body—a big smile on the face of Jesus.

Now, there are differences that exclude churches from the body of Christ. Jesus declared to be God. He said, "I and my Father are one"(John 10:30). Believing in the Trinity is a must. It is the most core and fundamental truth. Jesus can't just be a prophet or great person. He has to be God incarnate, the only begotten Son of God. The apostle Paul makes that point: "Concerning his Son Jesus Christ our Lord, which was made of the seed of David according to the flesh; and declared to be the Son of God with power, according to the spirit of holiness, by the resurrection from the dead" (Rom. 1:3–4). Jesus declared to be the Son of God and his proof was rising from the dead. The apostle John makes a similar point: "In the beginning was the word, and the word was with God, and the word was God . . . and the word was made flesh and dwelt among us, and we beheld his glory, the glory as of the only begotten of the Father" (John 1:1, 14). Jesus was with God and is God. This next verse says it best for me and was the first one I ever memorized almost thirty years ago: "And without controversy great is the mystery of godliness: God was manifest in the flesh, justified in the Spirit, seen of angels, preached unto the Gentiles, believed on in the world, received up into glory" (1 Tim. 3:16). It is a mystery so we don't have to understand it, but it's without controversy so we do have to believe it.

The other fundamental truth is that the shed blood of Jesus *alone* is the atonement for our sin. There is nothing that we can do to make ourselves right in God's eyes. "For by grace are you saved through faith, and not of yourselves: it is the gift of God. Not of works, lest any man should boast" (Eph. 2:8–9). The entire weight of our salvation rests upon the precious blood poured out for us at Calvary. Receiving what Jesus did for us is the only way to get to heaven and to see God. "Jesus said to him, I am the way, the truth, and the life; no man comes to the Father, but by me" (John 14:6).

Ephesians 1 talks about Christ's preeminence and ends by saying Jesus is the head of this body and what he says goes. What a healthy thing it would be for all of us to hold up our beliefs and traditions to the truth of God's Word. God is so gracious that if any of us didn't get it right and suddenly had an epiphany in understanding our errors and chose to do things the Lord's way, I believe God would visit us. God is patient and forgiving. He doesn't want anyone to die without him. "The Lord is not slack concerning his promise, as some men count slackness; but is long-suffering to us-ward, not willing that any should perish, but that all should come to repentance" (2 Peter 3:9). Jesus showed us the way by his example and that's the way we should do it.

I had to repent, believe Jesus to be the Son of God, and that his shed blood alone was the atonement for all my sins. So did every one else who's part of this body we call the church. God wants all of us, not just some of us. Jesus's way is the only way because he is the Way, the Truth, and the Life!

CHAPTER 8

THE DANGER: THE ENEMY

Many physical dangers exist that are able to destroy our health and kill us. We know that smoking can damage our respiratory system, alcohol can damage our organs, and steroids can ruin the rest of our body, not to mention incurable infectious diseases, toxic cancer-causing agents, and the list goes on and on. If that's not enough, the world around us can be equally as dangerous. If we allow ourselves to be in the wrong place at the wrong time, the results could be devastating. As hard as it is to believe, there are people that are ready to steal from us, defile us, and even kill us. The sad truth is that it happens every day.

Many dangers also lurk around us in the spiritual side of life. All this talk of getting strong in the Spirit is not just to show off our muscles. We're being trained to fight. It's more like basic training in the military than it is bodybuilding. I remember a certain popular cartoon in the early years of bodybuilding. A skinny boy at the beach was talking to a girl, and a big muscular guy came by, kicked sand on him, and then took the girl. After working out for a while, the skinny boy goes back to the beach, but now he's muscular. He kicks sand on the same guy and takes the girl back.

When God looks upon us, that's what he sees. When we are spiritually weak, the Enemy can push us around and beat us up. Our Father in heaven wants us strong in the spiritual realm so we can fight back and stick up for ourselves. Whether we want to believe it or not, we are involved in a spiritual fight. "For we wrestle not against flesh and blood, but against principalities . . . powers . . . rulers of the darkness . . . spiritual wickedness in high places" (Eph. 6:12). We wrestle against invisible things as Christians, so it can be very difficult to fight back.

My dear friends have a son who is a great high school wrestler here in Southern California. If you've ever seen a high school wrestling match, you'll notice two kids giving all they have to pin each other. This is a clear picture of what we're involved in, spiritually speaking. When we are weak, the Enemy has an easy time pinning us, and when we are strong in the Lord, we have an easy time pinning him. What you don't see in a high school match is a father running out of the stands to help his son beat the competitor, yet we're disappointed when God doesn't seem to help us. God is training us to have dominion over the Enemy. He is teaching us how to wrestle.

Many fiery trials come from the Enemy of our souls, a fallen world and society, issues that are common to man, our own irresponsibility, and our sinful nature, just to name a few. Every time we turn around, it seems like there's something else to wrestle with. We get a glimpse into this spiritual battle in the book of Daniel.

"Fear not Daniel, for from the first day . . . your words were heard, and I am come . . . but the Prince of Persia withstood me twenty-one days" (Dan. 10:12–13). Daniel didn't see any of this. He was just fasting and praying for God to do something, and yet the answer to his prayer was being contended for. It's like there is this very real world going on all around us, but it's invisible. But just like the world we live in, there are principles that rule it. All of God's training and everything Jesus taught us are to give us dominion in this world. We can't always see the benefit of some things in this world, but if we could see into this invisible world for just a second, it would all make sense.

Remember when Elisha's servant got up early one morning and noticed that the army of Syria had surrounded them while they slept? Elisha said, "Fear not, for they that be with us are more than they that be with them" (2 Kings 6:16). His servant wasn't seeing it. After all, it seemed to him as if it would be just two people against thousands of soldiers, horses, and chariots. "And Elisha prayed, and said 'Lord, open his eyes that he may see.' And the Lord opened the eyes of the young man; and he saw; and behold, the mountain was full of horses and chariots of fire round about" (2 Kings 6:17). This man's eyes were opened to the spiritual world around him, and suddenly the words of the prophet made sense.

If we could just see what goes on in the spiritual world all around us, things would be so much easier. We could see attacks coming and know just how to act. It's much harder when we can't see them coming. It forces us to be ready all the time. Jesus was always ready. When they brought the woman caught in adultery to him, he knew just what to say: "Let him that is without sin cast the first stone" (John 8:7). He was ready when Nicodemus came to him with questions and responded by saying, "You must be born again" (John 3:3). Jesus was always ready for the Pharisees with just the perfect answer.

Jesus showed us many examples of this invisible world. One of his favorite ways of showing this other world was through parables. He declares a very revealing truth in the parable of the sower. "To you it is given to know the mysteries of the kingdom of God, but to others in parables; that seeing they may not see, and hearing they might not understand" (Luke 8:10). Jesus is saying that even though he is making things easy to see and understand, people still won't get it. They compare what the Lord is saying to this world and can't believe that it could be such a big deal.

Take unforgiveness for instance. It doesn't seem like that big of a deal here. We don't go to jail because of it, and we can even cover it up and no one even knows that it lives in our hearts. But in this other world, unforgiveness is a huge big deal. Remember the parable of the unmerciful servant? The servant is forgiven a very big debt, but doesn't forgive his fellow servant for a much smaller debt. "And the Lord was wroth, and delivered him to the tormentors till he should pay all that was due. So likewise will My Heavenly Father do also unto you, if ye from your heart, forgive not everyone his brother his trespasses" (Matt. 18:34–35). It sure sounds like a big deal there. Jesus makes it even more intense in this Scripture: "But if you do not forgive men their trespasses, neither will your Father forgive your trespasses" (Matt. 6:15).

Suddenly, learning to forgive takes on a great weight of importance. If we are going to be strong in the spiritual world, we have to understand God's spiritual principles and live by them. The physical world's principles are easy to see. Take gravity for instance. If you throw a rock up in the air, it comes back to earth, or if you fill a balloon up with helium and let it go, it floats away. Gravity is easy to understand because you can see its effects. If you jump off a building and try to fly, you die—that's absolute. The spiritual world is the same. There are principles that rule it, and if we disregard them, we do it to our own peril.

The parable of the sower in Luke 8 is so revealing because Jesus literally explains how the spiritual world works: "Then comes the devil and takes it . . . in time of temptation fall away . . . choked with the pleasures of this life bringing no fruit to perfection" (Luke 8:12–14). The Lord is explaining to us that there is another world and there are things that go on in it that we can't see and don't understand. When we begin to understand this and our spiritual eyes open wide, we see an amazing battle that has been going on from the beginning of time.

"Be sober, be vigilant, because your adversary the devil, as a roaring lion, walks about, seeking whom he may devour" (1 Peter 5:8). The lion is the king of beasts and sits atop the food chain. Our Enemy is a formidable foe and not to be taken lightly. He wants to kill us and makes us dead to God and alive to him. He understands the principles of the spiritual world because that is where he lives. He knows that if he can get us to violate those principles, he can weaken us and even get a foothold to manipulate us.

The Scripture says, "Seeking whom he *may* devour." When we violate spiritual principles, we allow the Enemy access to our lives. Going back to the example of unforgiveness, even though we are the ones violated and didn't do anything wrong, when we harbor unforgiveness, we open ourselves up to the enemy's attacks because that is not allowed in this world.

We have to forgive because that is the essence of the one we serve. It's so easy to hold on to hurts and grudges and feel so justified because we didn't deserve to be hurt, and it wasn't fair. Our example should be Christ on the cross uttering those beautiful words to his Father concerning those that put him there, including us, for it was our sins that put Jesus on that cross. The Lord said, "Forgive them, for they know not what they do" (Luke 23:34).

Our Enemy is also a fisher of men. One of the dangers of sin is that he can hook us with temptation. Ultimately, that hook is a trap designed to keep us weak and steal our destiny. "He goes after her straightway, as an ox goes to the slaughter till a dart strike through his liver; as a bird hastens to the snare, knows not that it is for his life" (Prov. 7:22–23). What a perfect illustration: a stupid ox being led to the slaughterhouse where it is then killed. The ox thinks he is going for another fun, happy, little walk, and he doesn't even realize that his life is on the line.

Sin looks so appetizing and is often fun for a season, but it's designed to hurt us. Doing things contrary to the teachings of Jesus might be easier and satisfy our human passion, but sin is designed to destroy and damage us. The father of sin hates us because God loves us. This

Enemy is stalking us, waiting for a chance to pounce. Remember what Jesus said to Peter? "Simon, behold, Satan has desired to have you that he might sift to you as wheat" (Luke 22:31). This Enemy is sifting us, looking for something he can use. He is setting up situations for us to walk right into. These trials that we go through are not arbitrary, but have been designed specifically for us. He wants to steal our destiny and keep us from heaven.

But this battle is supposed to go both ways. "Lest Satan should get an advantage of us; for we are not ignorant of his devices" (2 Cor. 2:11). We should be learning his strategies from wrestling through the temptations we go through. He tempted Adam and Eve, and we can learn from that. He tempted Jesus, and we can definitely learn from that. The Lord's responses to the Enemy were always perfect, but Jesus is God and I'm not.

My wrestlings with the Enemy have been a little more hands on. When I became a believer at the age of twenty-six, I would slap myself in the face and say, "Stop it!" whenever a lustful situation raised its ugly head. Though that caught my attention at first, I knew there had to be a better way. I began to learn that I was fighting back when I would try to find someone to share my testimony with and invite them to receive the Lord. I would try to do things that would hurt Satan and his kingdom whenever he tried to tempt or hurt me. I was wrestling with the Enemy and winning with a transformed life. I could have thought to myself that God can't be real because I still deal with lust, or I'm such a bad sinner that I'll never change. I realized early on that I was in a fight, and that I had to learn to stick up for myself and continue to believe.

Our Scripture says to be vigilant. Now, I'm not saying that we look for the devil everywhere and that everything is the devil, but we should notice when things come against us and we start feeling more aggravated and anxious than usual. Instead of attacking the source, consider if this could be a spiritual assault and try praying and acting like Jesus teaches. It could instantly defuse everything and give us dominion to the point that we see it coming a mile away—a wrestling with the Enemy of our souls that leads to winning!

It's one thing to know we're in a fight, but it's another thing to know how to fight. Look at the apostle Paul. He and Silas were beaten and thrown in prison. "And at midnight Paul and Silas prayed and sang praises unto God . . . and immediately all the doors were opened, and everyone's bands were loosed" (Acts 16:12). Paul and Silas did the opposite of what the Enemy wanted them to do. The Enemy wanted them to look at the bloody mess they both were and the sewer of their inner prison and say that living for God really stinks. He wanted them to say, "I give up, and I'll never do anything for God again." But they didn't. Paul knew how to battle in the spiritual realm and shared that throughout the New Testament, giving us insight through his words and life.

Most of what we go through in our Christian walk is designed to make us strong in this arena, and insights we learn are to give us strategies to fight. Using the illustration of unforgiveness again, when someone hurts us we may use the expression "stabbed in the back." As long as we harbor unforgiveness, these swords and knives remain in our backs. We feel their pain and they affect everything that we do. By forgiving the person who stabbed you in the back, we actually pull the swords out.

If we could see into the spirit for just a second during this moment of forgiveness, it could be enlightening. Think of it like standing before the devil unarmed. When we forgive, we pull the swords out and now have a sword in each hand, ready to fight. The reason that we are armed before the Enemy ready to fight is that he wants to ruin relationships and poison us not to trust people, invest in people, or reach out to people. By forgiving we salvage the relationship, at least on our side, and become a living example of the power of forgiveness, encouraging others to likewise forgive. We wield a sword of forgiveness to hew the devil's kingdom.

For instance, every time the Pharisees saw Lazarus they wanted to kill him again because he was a walking, talking example of the power of Jesus. Or when David knocked Goliath down but couldn't cut off his head because he had no sword, so he pulled out Goliath's own sword and cut his head off with it. We use the Enemy's own devices against him. "For the weapons of our warfare are not carnal, but mighty through God to the pulling down of strongholds" (2 Cor. 10:4). Forgiveness is one of the most powerful weapons in our arsenal. The Enemy hates it because it destroys his kingdom.

As we seek to understand this invisible world and live by its principles, we learn to run, fight, and win. "I therefore so run, not as uncertainty; so fight I, not as one that beats the air" (1 Cor. 9:26). I don't want to be one that just closes his eyes and swings, but I want my punches to connect and have impact. We are in training to have dominion in the spiritual world, and like gladiators of old that had to fight to the death, we too have an arena of life where we have to perform. We are involved in a violent battle. "And from the days of John the Baptist until now the kingdom of heaven suffers violence, and the violent take it by force" (Matt. 11:12). We are being called as Christians to move forward, engage the Enemy, and take what is rightfully ours. We must take it by force. We are well able to take the land, let us go up at once and possess it!

By seeing into this world, we also notice that God is truly on our side. We understand that it's not God judging us when we violate these principles, but it's the consequences of our actions. Just like if we jumped out of a tree and break an ankle, it's not our parent's fault for telling us not to jump. It's our own fault for doing something stupid. Our parent's advice was to hopefully keep it from happening.

God is not a slave driver forcing us to live a certain way, but he is a concerned Father trying to protect us and make us strong. God's not the problem; he's the answer. "For God sent not His Son into the world to condemn the world; but that the world through Him might be saved. He that believes on Him is not condemned; but he that believes not is condemned already" (John 3:17–18). Our inability to be good enough to make heaven our home placed a death sentence upon our heads. "For all have sinned and come short of the glory of God" (Rom. 3:23). "There is none that doeth good, no, not one" (Rom. 3:12).

But God in his love and mercy made a way for us to enter into eternal life by giving us Jesus. "For God so loved the world that He gave His only begotten Son, that whosoever believeth in Him should not perish, but have everlasting life" (John 3:16). God is on our side. It's not about rules and regulations, but it's about love, friendship, and trust. Jesus showed us by his example, and he made the way. He loves us. "God is love" (1 John 4:6). Everything God does comes out of this. He wants the best for us, even when he corrects us.

Jesus has defeated hell, death, and the grave. He loves us and is training us to do the same. He's on our side rooting for us, and I can't wait to see him. I don't want the Enemy to be a danger to me; I want to be a danger to him. He's going to hell, while I'm going to heaven.

CHAPTER 9

THE ACCOMPLISHMENT: HEAVEN

One of the best achievements of physical training is a better quality of life. Being in shape and feeling good makes the hard work of training worth the time and effort invested. All of that hard work pays off, and we feel a sense of accomplishment. But those that train as part of an athletic team have their eyes on another prize. In baseball, it's the World Series. In football, it's the Super Bowl. In the Olympics, it's winning the gold medal. Great teams set aside their petty, individual differences and do what's best for the team so they can win the ultimate prize.

There are many rewards to our spiritual training as well: walking closely with Jesus and knowing him, battling our Enemy and winning, and of course, experiencing the peace that passes all understanding. But there is a great prize that we are all called to fix our gaze upon: heaven!

"By the appearing of our Lord Jesus Christ, who has abolished death and has brought life and immortality" (2 Tim. 1:10). Jesus came to give us life and immortality. We are immortal, and we are going to live forever. We should be walking around earth like we're afraid of nothing. Yes, our physical bodies will die, but our spirit never will. We shouldn't be timid with our opinions and insights, but instead we should boldly speak in love.

Jesus is the only way, and any opinion contrary to that will die with the speaker, because death has the final word—except with believers. "Death is swallowed up in victory. O death, where is thy sting?" (1 Cor. 15:54–55). Imagine not even being afraid to die? We would be fearless in everything we do, like all of the great men and women of God that have gone before us. They still exist, and they're looking down upon us, encouraging us to keep going. "Seeing we are compassed about with so great a cloud of witnesses . . . let us run the race that is set before us" (Heb. 12:1). Chapter 11 of Hebrews tells of the exploits of many of these great men and women of God. This Scripture says that they "compass" us about, like a football stadium filled to capacity. We are on the field running our race while the stands are full and the crowd is going wild, cheering us on and doing the wave. If we could quiet our spiritual ears, we could hear them speaking to us. "Go for it! You won't regret it! This place is awesome!"

Someday we will join them. "And the dead shall be raised incorruptible . . . and this mortal must put on immortality" (1 Cor. 15:52–53). Just imagine how wonderful it's going to be to see our Father in heaven and realize all that he did to get us there. Or to see Jesus face-to-face and feel his presence and all that love. Or to see the Holy Spirit and understand all that he did on earth to help us. Or to speak with Moses, the apostle Paul, or King David and all his mighty men. We will have finished our race and finally be in paradise for all of eternity. God wants us to encourage one another with heaven.

We can't always encourage each other in difficult situations that never seem to change, or those very painful times that are beyond consolation. We can offer sympathy, but that does little to encourage. Sometimes the only thing that can help us is to have an eternal perspective and to realize that there is more to life than just what is here on earth.

Peter says that things can be hard here and a heaviness exists that can come upon us. It can feel like we're going through the fire, but at the same time something beautiful is being created. "You are in heaviness through manifold temptations. That the trial of your faith being much more precious than gold that perishes, though it be tried with fire" (1 Peter 1:6–7). It can be very difficult to see the good things God is doing in us while we're going through those hard times. When we have no food and no shelter, when family members and loved ones are enduring life-threatening illnesses, when we're being ostracized because of our faith, or through a million other situations, we often fail to believe that something beautiful is being created, but it is.

As we make godly choices to trust and continue to love and believe God, an aspect of Christ is being formed in us. Trails are like the aggravating sand that gets into an oyster shell that, in the end, turns into a beautiful pearl. Peter also speaks to these beautiful struggles: "An inheritance incorruptible, and undefiled, and that fades not away, reserved in Heaven for you" (1 Peter 1:4). He is saying that we have a reservation to a place so great that it makes it all worth it.

Yes, the trials are real, and yes, the trials are painful, but they are producing something amazing. It's like working out at the gym. The more difficult and painful the training is, the greater the muscle growth will be. This is where the phrase "No pain, no gain" began. Amazing gains in muscle size and strength come from the excruciating pain of heavy weight lifting. With much pain often comes much gain.

Peter sees precious gold being formed in us and doesn't focus as much on the painful trials we're going through. For example, when a glaring, bright sun burns our eyes, we put on sunglasses. Everything looks better, but in reality the only thing that has changed is the way we're now viewing the situation. We need to cultivate an eternal perspective and learn how to view everything through the eyes of heaven.

The apostle Paul says that these sufferings are creating something so beautiful in us that the ultimate results can't even compare with the challenging process it took to get there. "For I reckon that the sufferings of this present time are not worthy to be compared with the glory, which shall be revealed in us" (Rom. 8:18). Everything we go through is making us who we will be for all of eternity. We're being conformed into the image of Christ, and the closer we get to that, the more amazing we will be for all of eternity. In the previous verse, Paul reveals our ultimate reward: "Heirs of God, and joint heirs with Christ" (Rom. 8:17). He is saying that we get everything

Jesus gets, namely, spending eternity with God the Father and everything that goes with that. Paul is essentially saying, "How can anything we go through here on earth compare to that?" He provides us with an eternal perspective.

"Though our outward man perish, yet the inward man is renewed day by day. For our light affliction, which is but for a moment, works in us a far more exceeding and eternal weight of glory" (2 Cor. 4:16–18). Paul is saying that these afflictions are creating something of eternal weight and glory that won't be revealed until we get to Heaven. It blows my mind when I consider that the apostle Paul is the one writing this.

In 2 Corinthians 11:23–33, we read about some of Paul's afflictions. I have personally gone through many difficult and painful situations, and the only solace I could find was in reading those verses and thinking to myself that if Paul could endure what he did, then God could help me too. Let's read some of this scripture: "in stripes above measure, in prison more frequent, in deaths oft . . . five times received forty stripes save one, thrice beaten with rods, once stoned, thrice suffered shipwreck, a night and a day I have been in the deep . . . in weariness and painfulness . . . in cold and nakedness." Five times Paul received thirty-nine lashes like Jesus did before going to the cross, ripping his back wide open with blood everywhere. They later stoned him to death, and after they dragged his dead body out of town, God raised him from the dead. He felt every stone hitting him until he died. He spent twenty-four hours floating in the middle of the ocean, probably after one of his shipwrecks. Paul calls all of that light afflictions that last but a moment. Paul sees what we do not, and he tells us about it a few verses later.

"How that he was caught up into paradise, and heard unspeakable words, which it is not lawful for a man to utter (The Third Heaven)" (2 Cor. 12:4). Paul knew someone or had a vision that was in heaven, and it made everything he went through seem like nothing. As a result of Paul's glimpse of heaven, he's basically saying, "You can't even compare what I went through to what awaits me." Understanding the reality of heaven is the key to being greatly encouraged.

Jesus wants to encourage us with heaven. "Let not your heart be troubled . . . in My Father's house are many mansions; if it were not so, I would have told you. I go to prepare a place for you . . . that where I am, you shall be also" (John 14:1–3). Jesus spoke this right after telling Peter of his betrayal and right before Judas arrived with guards to apprehend him. All hell was about to break loose, including Jesus's trial, scourging, and crucifixion. Still, the Lord's main concern was that his followers would not lose heart, but would understand what awaited them. Living for Jesus can be so hard, and knowing that we have a final destination called Paradise, where we will spend eternity with the Lord himself, can really help our present circumstances if we actually believe it. The Lord says if it were not so I would have told you. In other words, Jesus isn't making this up. Heaven actually exists. Heaven is real, God is real, and our faith is real.

Heaven is a place of rejoicing, worshiping the Lamb of God, rest from all our labors and battles, receiving crowns and rewards, the bride being married, and everyone being comforted. "And God shall wipe away all tears from their eyes, and there shall be no more death . . . sorrow . . . crying . . . pain, for the former things are passed away" (Rev. 21:4). God is personally going to comfort us. The same finger that wrote the Ten Commandments on tablets of stone is going to wipe away every tear from our eyes. It's so amazing to even think about that. The Lord can't wait to comfort us. The story of Lazarus the beggar is a perfect example. Lazarus has a tough life, the rich man has an easy life, but then they both die. "And it came to pass that the beggar died, and was carried by the angels into Abraham's bosom: the rich man also died, and was buried; and in hell he lift up his eyes, being in torments" (Luke 16:22–23).

One of the greatest things about heaven is that it's the better of the two choices. No, we don't come back as animals, and there is no purgatory. Jesus died so we could spend eternity with him, but also to save us from hell, another very real place. In the parable of the sheep and goats, there was a judgment. "Depart from me, ye cursed, into everlasting fire, prepared for the devil and his angels" (Matt. 25:41). So many Christians have used the reality of hell in trying to manipulate people into a decision by saying, "You'd better get saved or you're going to hell." When we hear that, we might think to ourselves, "Where's the love?" The truth of the matter is that our choice leads to a sobering reality: we are going to spend eternity in one of two places. The choices we make and the life we live will determine our fate. My dear mom passed away while I was in the middle of writing this final chapter on heaven. She was such a wonderful, loving person, and anyone that knew her loved her. She will be greatly missed. I loved my mom. Her passing helps me to realize the reality of life and death. It's not just a Sunday school story of the sweet bye and bye. Death is an actual appointment to which every one of us must eventually succumb. "It is appointed unto men once to die, but after this the judgment" (Heb. 9:27). Heaven is there for all of us to choose because Jesus died to purchase it for us. It is so wonderful to be seen that one glimpse of it makes going through hell on earth well worth it, and yet failing to choose Jesus on this side of eternity separates us from it on the other side.

"And they rest not day and night, saying: 'Holy, Holy, Holy, Lord God Almighty, which was, and is, and is to come . . .' The four and twenty elders fall down before Him that sat on the throne and worshiped Him that lives forever and ever, and cast their crowns before the throne, saying, 'You are worthy, O Lord, to receive glory, and honor, and power; for you have created all things, and for your pleasure they are created'" (Rev. 4:8–11).

"And I beheld, and I heard the voice of many angels round about the throne . . . and elders, and the number of them was 10,000 times 10,000, and thousands of thousands; saying with a loud voice, 'Worthy is the Lamb that was slain to receive power, and riches, and wisdom, and strength, and honor, and glory, and blessing'" (Rev. 5:11–12).

"And the spirit and the bride say, 'Come.' And let him that hears say, 'Come.' And let him that is athirst come. And whoever so will, let him take of the water of life freely . . . He that testifies these things says, 'Surely I come quickly.' Amen. Even so, come, Lord Jesus" (Rev. 22:17–20).

**Heaven is our home, and
we will live forever!**

In Closing: Hope

It's not always easy being a believer. We are outnumbered by unbelievers and made to feel foolish for trusting in something that no one has ever seen, but that's faith. No one is perfect, and when we make mistakes they're magnified. We're made to feel like hypocrites, but God has grace. We think of what we should be and then look at what we are. Sometimes we may even think to ourselves, "What's the use?" But God is leading us.

We are being molded into great men and women of God and we can't even see it, but God is doing it. We are fighting the good fight of faith, and God is proud of us. He wants us to look toward the future with hope and to press into him to see all he has for us. "Brethren, I count not myself to have apprehended; but this one thing I do, forgetting those things which are behind, and reaching forth unto those things which are before. I press toward the mark for the prize of the high calling of God in Jesus Christ" (Phil. 3:13–14). Everything that is behind me is behind me. It's the past and it's gone. The only thing that remains from the past is what I've learned from it. Today is a new beginning, and my eyes are focused on the Lord, to be a part of whatever he wants to do.

We need a strong desire to walk in love, forgiveness, and the power of his Spirit. We need unity with our brothers and sisters and to fearlessly share the gospel. Allowing God to lead us without any agenda and being open to whatever he would ask us to do—this is what I want to do. I want to live for God and be alive to God. I want to give it everything I've got until there's nothing left because that's what Jesus did for me!

Thank you Jesus. I love you.

I Had a Dream

Like Ezekiel, I stood on a mountainside looking upon a valley of dry bones. The angel said, "These are the people who once believed but walked away and have become spiritually dead." I saw those who were hurt by churches, those who felt let down by God, and those who gave up because of the appetites of their own flesh.

The angel then said to me, "Can these bones live"? I said, "Yes, I know they can live, because I was one of them." Then he asked me to prophesy over them and I did, and the breath of God entered them. We stood up, and I saw an exceedingly great army as far as the eye could see stand with me.

I had another dream. I saw Jesus high in the sky, dying on the cross. Below, I saw every different church denomination. The churches had all constructed walls to keep certain people in and certain others out, and as I beheld, blood and tears began falling from the Lord's cross, dripping on these walls. Suddenly, the walls melted until they had vanished. The people came out nervous at first, but when they saw how much they had in common they began to embrace, and as I beheld they all came together and stood upon their feet. They were as big as the earth.

I had yet one more dream. All of humanity noticed the giant church and the army of redeemed believers and came running. They were lame and disfigured at first, but the closer they got, the more they became whole. As I looked around, I saw the greatest revival that had ever taken place, and we were in the very middle of it. Then someone turned to me and said, "This must be heaven on earth." Suddenly, we all heard a trumpet blast and looked up—it was the Lord! He had returned just like he said he would.

I had a dream . . . and then it happened! (Prophetically speaking)

In Jesus Name,
Amen!

About the Author

As a pastor and assistant pastor, Mark Foley gained great insight into God's desire to spiritually strengthen all believers. As a personal trainer and fitness instructor, Mark understands the way our bodies build strength. When he began to see the striking similarities between physical training and spiritual fitness, Mark became greatly encouraged and strengthened in God. He lives in Southern California where his greatest joy is spending time and talking with his children and watching them grow into all that God has destined them to be.

Printed in the United States
By Bookmasters